AIR UNIVERSITY

SCHOOL OF ADVANCED AIR AND SPACE STUDIES

Intelligence and Design

Thinking about Operational Art

BRIAN J. TYLER
Lieutenant Colonel, USAF

Drew Paper No. 14

Air University Press
Air Force Research Institute
Maxwell Air Force Base, Alabama

Project Editor
Belinda L. Bazinet

Copy Editor
Carolyn J. Burns

Cover Art, Book Design, and Illustrations
Daniel Armstrong

Composition and Prepress Production
Vivian D. O'Neal

Print Preparation and Distribution
Diane Clark

AIR FORCE RESEARCH INSTITUTE

AIR UNIVERSITY PRESS

Director and Publisher
Allen G. Peck

Editor in Chief
Oreste M. Johnson

Managing Editor
Demorah Hayes

Design and Production Manager
Cheryl King

Air University Press
155 N. Twining St., Bldg. 693
Maxwell AFB, AL 36112-6026
afri.aupress@us.af.mil

Disclaimer

Opinions, conclusions, and recommendations expressed or implied within are solely those of the authors and do not necessarily represent the official policy or position of the organizations with which they are associated or the views of the School of Advanced Air and Space Studies, Air Force Research Institute, Air University, United States Air Force, Department of Defense, or any other US government agency. This publication is cleared for public release and unlimited distribution.

AFRI AU PRESS
AIR FORCE RESEARCH INSTITUTE

The Drew Papers

The Drew Papers are award-winning master's theses selected for publication by the School of Advanced Air and Space Studies (SAASS), Maxwell AFB, Alabama. This series of papers commemorates the distinguished career of Col Dennis "Denny" Drew, USAF, retired. In 30 years at Air University, Colonel Drew served on the Air Command and Staff College faculty, directed the Airpower Research Institute, and served as dean, associate dean, and professor of military strategy at SAASS. Colonel Drew is one of the Air Force's most extensively published authors and an international speaker in high demand. He has lectured to over 100,000 students at Air University as well as to foreign military audiences. In 1985 he received the Muir S. Fairchild Award for outstanding contributions to Air University. In 2003 Queen Beatrix of the Netherlands made him a Knight in the Order of Orange-Nassau for his contributions to education in the Royal Netherlands Air Force.

The Drew Papers are dedicated to promoting the understanding of air and space power theory and application. These studies are published by the Air University Press and broadly distributed throughout the US Air Force, the Department of Defense, and other governmental organizations, as well as to leading scholars, selected institutions of higher learning, public-policy institutes, and the media.

Please send inquiries or comments to

Commandant and Dean
School of Advanced Air and Space Studies
125 Chennault Circle
Maxwell AFB, AL 36112
Tel: (334) 953-5155
DSN: 493-5155
saass.admin@us.af.mil

Contents

Foreword

Since its formal articulation by the American armed forces in the 1980s, operational art has been more written about than understood. The present author, Lt Col Brian Tyler, does not make that mistake. He combines an insightful mind and a rigorous system of inquiry with a wealth of experience as an intelligence officer. These attributes lead him to a number of useful and important insights concerning the practice of the intelligence craft in this important arena of military activity where warriors struggle to reconcile the gritty problems that bubble up from tactical reality with the grand designs that cascade down from strategic desiderata.

Tyler synthesizes two approaches to his project that significantly enrich his investigation—one historical, the other conceptual. The principal evidence comes from the Malayan Emergency of 1948–1960, with a particular focus on the intelligence needs and methods of the British high commissioner, Sir Gerald Templer. Digging deeply into the documentation of the anticommunist conflict, Tyler convincingly demonstrates—though careful not to claim too much for—the important role of effective information gathering and analysis in bringing about the ultimate British victory.

The big idea of the thesis comes from the emerging discipline of design. Tyler works through a large body of thought to reduce design to its essence— "a highly complex mental process that imagines the future, reflects on the past, and produces an understanding of both the problem and the optimal solution." Operational design then simply becomes the application of this construct in the conduct of operational art.

Next, the author takes a leaf from Carl von Clausewitz's third step of critical analysis, criticism proper, and retrospectively applies the rubric of early twenty-first century design to the conduct of the mid-twentieth century campaign in Malaya. This leads to the intriguing argument that although Templer and his intelligence professionals did not—indeed could not—consciously use design as a methodology, they intuitively grasped and applied its essence. The work concludes with some well-reasoned suggestions as to how contemporary commanders and their intelligence staffs, emulating Templer and his aides, can use design constructs to help them pierce the fog of war and impose their wills on an uncooperative adversary.

Colonel Tyler's "Intelligence and Design: Thinking about Operational Art" received the Air University Foundation's Award for Best SAASS Security Studies Thesis of 2011. It stands as a model for all who believe that military thought and practice can be advanced by inspired scholarship.

Harold R. Winton

Harold R. Winton
Professor of Military History and Theory
School of Advanced Air and Space Studies

About the Author

Lt Col Brian J. Tyler is an intelligence officer who has served in various assignments in the US Air Force and US intelligence community. He graduated from the US Air Force Academy in 1996 and holds advanced degrees from the University of Maryland's School of Public Affairs and Air University's School of Advanced Air and Space Studies.

Acknowledgments

Most worthwhile projects involve the contributions of many, and this paper is no exception. I owe my gratitude to several for their assistance, encouragement, and inspiration.

Foremost, I am indebted to our nation and Air Force in many ways, including the gift of spending a year at SAASS to study and think about matters important to our national security.

I will be forever grateful to Dr. Harold R. Winton, my thesis advisor, for his professionalism and commitment to my development as an officer and scholar. Dr. Winton is a true gentleman whom I am honored to call mentor and friend. While he granted me the latitude to make this project my own, he also guided every aspect of it. To the extent this paper is readable—much less should it be useful—it is because of Dr. Winton's insight, persistence, and patience. It is a distinct (and sometimes daunting) privilege at SAASS to study with Dr. Winton. I thank him for choosing me to become a "Wintonian scholar," and I hope this work and my service prove to be worthy of his investment.

I am also thankful to Dr. Stephen E. Wright for his assistance with multiple facets of this project. He knows strategy and campaign planning and has an uncanny knack for making the obtuse appear obvious. Dr. Wright was an invaluable resource as I studied the nuances of operational design. Additionally, as my reader, his attention to detail improved the overall quality of this work. I also appreciate the aid of Dr. James D. Kiras in making sense of the Malayan Emergency. He was gracious with his time, and his recommendations of key works on the subject helped guide my research.

For the curious, research is a peculiar endeavor that never seems to end. The wonderful and patient professionals at the Air University and US Air Force Academy libraries helped me manage my quest for sources. In particular, I am thankful for the assistance of Mrs. Sandhya Malladi and Dr. Mary Ruwell.

To the faculty and staff of SAASS, thank you for your commitment to our country, our Air Force, and the students of this superb institution. As well, to my colleagues of SAASS Class XX: "Stay Thirsty!" I learned much from each of you and I am grateful to have walked this path together. It will be an honor to serve alongside you in the years ahead.

The military intelligence community is a fascinating world filled with extraordinary and selfless men and women who continually shun the spotlight but never the yoke of protecting our nation. To my many mentors and friends who continue to shape my understanding of our profession I say simply thank you. I hope this paper represents you well.

Finally, words cannot describe how much I appreciate my family and their support. I am in constant wonderment at the exceptionalism and resilience of my wife and children. Their love, loyalty, and joy continually remind me just how blessed I am. It is to them I dedicate this project and the past 11 months.

Despite the assistance of those mentioned above, this work remains imperfect. All of the errors and limitations of this paper are mine alone.

Abstract

Uncertainty is an inescapable part of war that stems, in part, from war's "wicked" problems and the complex, adaptive systems that produce them. While uncertainty in war is chronic, both operational intelligence and operational design endeavor to mitigate it on behalf of the commander. Operational intelligence strives to make sense of past and current circumstances to inform future action; operational design tries to shape the future based on what is learned from the past and known or suspected about the present. Operational intelligence collects and analyzes information to build understanding of a complex situation; operational design translates understanding into an approach for achieving operational aims and strategic outcomes. Without uncertainty in war, there would be no need for operational intelligence or operational design; because of uncertainty, they become two sides of the same coin.

This paper is about intelligence at the operational level of war. It is also about operational design and the 1948–60 anticommunist counterinsurgency known as the Malayan Emergency. Using a dialectic approach, the paper evaluates how operational intelligence should be influenced by emerging concepts of operational design. It analyzes the essence and practice of operational intelligence, considers the commander's role in operational intelligence, and assesses intelligence contributions in the Malayan Emergency. Next it examines operational design, including a design-based reassessment of the Malayan Emergency. Finally, the paper synthesizes studies of operational intelligence and operational design to produce insights and suggestions for commanders and intelligence professionals on performing, educating, training, and equipping operational intelligence.

The project concludes that operational intelligence is more than tactical reconnaissance writ large. It suggests ways to balance the inherent tensions of operational intelligence—those between the strategic and tactical and between collection and analysis—that will improve the effectiveness of the joint force. The project also concludes that operational intelligence and operational design are complementary cognitive processes that, together, can enrich operational art in the information age.

Chapter 1

Introduction

Uncertainty is a hallmark of war. Richard K. Betts, a leading scholar in the field of intelligence, wrote, "It is the role of intelligence to extract certainty from uncertainty and to facilitate coherent decision [*sic*] in an incoherent environment."[1] Complexity theory also informs the complicated decisions of joint force commanders. Recognizing the extreme interconnectedness of our world and of our battlespaces is a crucial first step in coherent thinking.[2] However, identifying, analyzing, and forecasting the political, military, economic, social, infrastructural, and informational factors and linkages of complex, adaptive systems are not simple.

This paper is about intelligence of a certain kind. It is not concerned with the intelligence of a given mind studied by psychologists. Rather, it focuses on the kind of intelligence a commander must have to design and execute plans—the intelligence relevant to security.[3]

The practice of intelligence involves two central functions that seek to demystify complex problems for commanders—collection and analysis.[4] Collection gathers information essential to effective decision making. However, collection alone is insufficient because the implications of much of the evidence gathered in war are ambiguous. Concerted thinking about the adversary and operational environment is also necessary. Exploring the relationship between collection, analysis, and decision making in a complex environment is the overarching purpose of this paper.

To the extent that collection and analysis are separable, the former seems to bedazzle actors of the information age. The complicated venture of intelligence, surveillance, and reconnaissance (ISR) is the product of what some refer to as a revolution in military affairs. In 1995 Adm William Owens, then vice chairman of the US Joint Chiefs of Staff, anticipated that a system of systems with the potential to transform modern warfare would emerge from the convergence of military practices and technologies.[5] Today, increasingly powerful ISR capabilities can discern very small objects and momentary events. As one author predicted, we are witnessing the "disappearance of disappearance."[6]

Consequently, the promise of technology draws commanders and their directors of intelligence toward constructing an ideal-type brilliant battlespace in which networked sensors illuminate the arena and penetrate the fog of war.[7] Commanders yearn to make informed decisions, so accurate discernment in the midst of uncertainty is the intelligence professional's business. To this end, as part of the modern command, control, communications, computers, and intelligence system, intelligence leaders strive to design and direct a panoptic "mesh" or "surveillant assemblage" that peers through the twilight to describe the operational environment, divine the adversary's capabilities and intentions, and achieve a decisive advantage in battlespace knowledge.[8]

Nevertheless, uncertainty in war remains a persistent and perverse reality. Where does it come from? Werner Heisenberg's uncertainty principle stated that ambiguity is always present in the perceptible realm.[9] The Prussian sage Carl von Clausewitz attributed uncertainty to the free will of the adversary and the inherent limitations of the human mind.[10] Claude Shannon, the founder of information theory, identified "information overload" as a noisy source of uncertainty.[11] Thomas Kuhn indicted the limits of human cognition as the cause of incomplete understanding.[12] Robert Jervis argued that cognitive biases limit accurate perception.[13] At the center of warfare and uncertainty are human beings, in all their power and frailty.

The variety of potential human choices makes war a complex and dynamic endeavor. The Chinese theorist Sun Tzu said, "Now in war there may be one hundred changes in each step."[14] Despite even great efforts of collection and analysis, there will always be residual uncertainty.[15] This is why the military historian Martin van Creveld described war as an "irrational business par excellence."[16]

Most commanders and intelligence professionals recognize the brilliant battlespace and perfect knowledge as being types of fata morgana. Intelligence cannot achieve omniscience, nor can it prophesy the future. Rather, it is a thoughtful endeavor to reduce the number of times a commander is surprised.[17] The intractable inadequacy of intelligence requires a necessary degree of fatalism among warriors.[18] Nevertheless, forecasts remain helpful and may provide a significant advantage in the complicated enterprise of war.

Theories on systems and complexity help explain the character of the universe, including its wars and battlespaces. Scholarship on the complexity of systems has recently emerged from an improved understanding of and tolerance for uncertainty. For centuries, the reductive approaches of scientific research and rational thought illuminated the world's constituent parts.[19] Understanding the interactions among those parts is the aim of complexity theory. Albert-Laszlo Barabasi wrote, "Today we increasingly recognize that nothing happens in isolation. Most events and phenomena are connected, caused by, and interacting with a huge number of other pieces of a complex universal puzzle."[20]

M. Mitchell Waldrop defined complex systems as those in which "a great many independent agents are interacting with each other in a great many ways."[21] With each interaction, the agents adapt, responding to environmental stimuli. According to Waldrop this imbues complex adaptive systems with "a kind of dynamism that makes them qualitatively different from static objects."[22]

As we recognize and understand the interconnectedness of our world, we enlarge and adjust explanatory models that inform decision making. However, the more we know, the more we realize that our understanding of our ever-changing universe is incomplete. Additionally, as information-age technology compresses space and time, it increases the scale and pace of interactivity and change.[23] While the world has always been complex, both enhanced understanding of it and advancing technology contribute to our perceptions of increasing complexity.

How is complexity understood? Waldrop argues that interdisciplinary approaches lift the shroud of complexity best.[24] Intelligence study has a rich history and growing literature on analysis and decision support in the midst of ambiguity. Similarly, a more recent discourse on operational design presents techniques for commanders and planners to cope with uncertainty and complexity.

Operational design emerged when military thinkers began applying insights from the multidisciplinary literature of design to the operational art of war. Operational design is a nonlinear and iterative process intended to help commanders develop operational approaches by aiding their understanding of the complex environments in which they operate and the complex problems they face. Like their intelligence counterparts, designers work to mitigate the uncertainty that surrounds the commander. This shared purpose leads to the project's central question: How should the practice of intelligence at the operational level of war be influenced by emerging concepts of operational design?

The superstructure of this paper is a simple dialectic between intelligence and design at the operational level of war. The study proceeds through five logical steps. Its initial stage—comprised of the first three chapters—examines operational intelligence, including its essence, practice, and relationship with the principal decision maker—the commander. Chapter 2 begins by exploring the essence of intelligence through an examination of its various definitions. Next, it considers the emergence of the operational level of war in military thought. Finally, it synthesizes intelligence and war's operational level to propose a definition of operational intelligence. This chapter draws from theory, a range of secondary sources and American joint military doctrine. Because scholarship on operational intelligence is relatively sparse, the first three chapters transfer numerous insights from a substantially larger body of work on strategic intelligence.[25]

Chapter 3 examines the practice of intelligence at the operational level of war. It begins by describing the characteristics of operational intelligence, including its purposes, consumers, processes, and products. It then distills the activities of operational intelligence into its two most central functions—collection and analysis. The chapter supplements its references to US joint military doctrine with sources from the intelligence literature.[26]

The fourth chapter considers the relationship between the operational-level commander and intelligence. It examines the attributes of commanders and intelligence advisors that contribute to the successful conduct of intelligence. It also highlights the central role of the commander in the employment of intelligence. The chapter leans heavily on two works edited by the historian and military intelligence scholar Michael Handel.[27]

The second stage of the paper assesses empirical evidence of the interaction between intelligence and the formulation of operational concepts by examining the historical example of the 1948–60 anticommunist counterinsurgency known as the Malayan Emergency. Chapter 5 begins with a brief overview of the emergency that identifies key events, decisions, and leaders. In this early section, the chapter diverges slightly from existing scholarship by presenting a new periodization that coincides with changes in British strategy. Next, the chapter considers the evolution of collection and analysis relative to those periods. It also spotlights the successes, failures, structures, and key relationships of intelligence during the emergency. Sources for this chapter include several primary and secondary works. It references multiple British government documents found in A. J. Stockwell's helpful compilation.[28] Among the most influential secondary sources were Riley Sunderland's 1964 report; books by Richard Clutterbuck, Karl Hack, and John Cloake; and Cloake's biography.[29] By the chapter's end, the reader will understand what operational intelligence is, how it supports multiple customers including the commander, and how it influences the development of the operational concept.

The project next analyzes operational design to include its essence, practice, and relationship with the commander. Chapter 6 evaluates the essence of operational design by first regarding the concept from which it evolved. It begins by explaining the relationship between uncertainty and complexity using concepts from systems theory, which is the theoretical foundation of design. It then examines the complexity of social systems and their so-called "wicked" problems. Finally, it outlines the process of design and evaluates its utility in managing uncertainty and complexity. Chapter 6 extracts material from various sources on systems theory, complexity, and design.[30]

Chapter 7 evaluates operational design as a theoretical construct. It first sketches the concept's origin and background and then defines and distinguishes it from planning at the operational level of war. It assesses the method's five steps—environmental framing, problem framing, operational approach development, documentation, and reframing—and considers the roles of the commander and the design team in the process. This chapter consults several US joint and US Army planning sources.[31] An additional trove of insight was the collection of student theses, primarily from the School of Advanced Military Studies, that explore various aspects of operational design.

Chapter 8, the project's fourth stage, reassesses the Malayan Emergency using the concepts of operational design. It evaluates the development of an understanding of the emergency's context and central problem by two commanders, which informed the creation and continuation of a successful operational approach. It also considers their collaborative leadership styles during the process. It then examines the composition of one commander's design team. By its conclusion, the reader will better appreciate operational design, how it supports the commander, and how it influences the development of the operational concept.

Chapter 9 constitutes the project's final stage. It synthesizes the insights gained from the conceptual and evidentiary assessments of intelligence with the insights gained from studying operational design to produce a conclusion as to how emerging concepts of operational design should influence the practice of operational-level intelligence. The sources for this chapter are mostly the same as those used throughout the project. However, a handful of additional works proved useful in refining the argument.[32]

The project's final chapter summarizes its major conclusions and presents several implications of this research for the education, training, equipping, and employment of operational intelligence in the information age.

The main ambition of this project is to help commanders and intelligence professionals improve the effectiveness of operations through the optimal employment of intelligence at the operational level of war. If it contributes toward a more comprehensive understanding of operational intelligence, it will be successful. In doing so, it will also add a small token to the relatively limited discourse on operational intelligence.

The project also aims to bridge the emerging scholarships on operational intelligence and operational design, two potentially complementary cognitive processes intended to aid commanders in the effective conduct of operations and campaigns. Little research exists on the role of intelligence in operational design. Connecting these literatures may expand our understanding of both concepts.

A tertiary goal is to shed new light on the ingredients of success in the Malayan Emergency, especially the role played by intelligence. While the evidence marshaled in chapter 5 should enrich the reader's understanding of operational intelligence, it may also shape the understanding of how intelligence affected the decisions of Lt Gen Sir Harold Briggs and Gen Sir Gerald Templer. To my knowledge, a previous analysis of the Malayan Emergency through the rubric of operational design does not exist. Chapter 8 may contribute in a small way to the literature on Malaya and to that on operational design.

Notes

All notes appear in shortened form. For full details, see the appropriate entry in the bibliography.

1. Betts, "Analysis, War, and Decision," 69.

2. Nelson, *Computer Lib*. Nelson described the information-age world as "intertwingled" because of its extreme interconnectedness.

3. Kent, *Strategic Intelligence*, vii. Kent was a former chairman of the Central Intelligence Agency's Office of National Estimates and a founding father of the American intelligence community. This paragraph paraphrases Kent's similar caveat on the kind of intelligence discussed in his book. While Kent's focus was strategic intelligence and the strategist, this project regards operational intelligence and the commander.

4. Ibid., 4. Kent divided intelligence operations into surveillance and research. This paper uses the contemporary terms collection and analysis.

5. Owens, "Emerging System of Systems," 15.

6. Haggerty and Ericson, "Surveillant Assemblage," 619.

7. Arnett, "Welcome to Hyperwar," 15; and Libicki, "Information War," 411–28. The "brilliant battlespace" is an ideal-type operational area fully illuminated by information-age technologies to achieve a level of omniscience in and perfect understanding of that battlespace. The term differs from the "brilliant weapons" described by Arnett. Arnett's weapons are "crewless tanks, cruise missiles that behave like kamikaze robots, advanced air-defense missiles, and anti-missile satellites" and those machines that will "carry out battle decisions independent of their human counterparts." While autonomy from humans characterizes *brilliant* (i.e., intelligent) *weapons*, the *brilliant* (i.e., illuminated) *battlespace* informs human decision making. As such, my use of the term more closely resembles Libicki's term "battlespace illumination."

8. Libicki, *Mesh and the Net*; and Haggerty and Ericson, "Surveillant Assemblage," 605–22.

9. Heisenberg, *Physical Principles*, 13–19.

10. Clausewitz, *On War*, 137–40.

11. Shannon, "A Mathematical Theory," 379–423, 623–56.

12. Kuhn, *Structure of Scientific Revolutions*.

13. Jervis, *Perception and Misperception*.

14. Sun Tzu, *Illustrated Art of War*, 124.

15. Pateman, *Residual Uncertainty*, 175–84.

16. Van Creveld, *Command in War*, 16.

17. Johnson, *Secret Agencies*, 141.

18. Betts, "Analysis, War, and Decision," 89.

19. Barabasi, *Linked*, 6.

20. Ibid., 7.

21. Waldrop, *Complexity*, 11.

22. Ibid., 11–12.

23. Friedman, *The World Is Flat,* 8–10.

24. Waldrop, *Complexity,* 67.

25. Thomas, "U.S. Military Intelligence Analysis,"138–54. The book gives an explanation of the lack of military intelligence scholarship.

26. Betts, "Analysis, War, and Decision," 61–89; May, *Knowing One's Enemies*; Nye, "Peering into the Future," 82–93; and Heuer, *Psychology of Intelligence Analysis.*

27. Handel, *Leaders and Intelligence*; and Handel, *Intelligence and Military Operations.*

28. Stockwell, *British Documents on the End of Empire.*

29. Sunderland, "Antiguerrilla Intelligence in Malaya"; Clutterbuck, *The Long Long War*; Cloake, *Templer*; Coates, *Suppressing Insurgency*; and Hack, "British Intelligence and Counter-Insurgency," 124–55.

30. Checkland, *Systems Thinking*; Rittel and Webber, "Dilemmas in a General Theory," 155–69; and Lawson, *How Designers Think.*

31. Naveh, *In Pursuit of Military Excellence*; Ryan, *Art of Design*; Schmitt, "A Systemic Concept"; and Kem, *Design.*

32. Murray and Millett, *Military Effectiveness*; Rosen, *Winning the Next War*; Bousquet, *Scientific Way of Warfare*; and Senge, *Fifth Discipline.*

Chapter 2

Intelligence at the Operational Level of War

Now the reason the enlightened prince and the wise general conquer the enemy whenever they move and their achievements surpass those of other men is foreknowledge.

—Sun Tzu
The Art of War

The pursuit of superior intelligence is as old as war. The prominent military historian Martin van Creveld concluded, "From Plato to NATO, the history of command in war consists essentially of an endless quest for certainty."[1] This quest for battlespace awareness actually predates Plato. Moses and Joshua commissioned spies before the Israelite invasion of Canaan, and Sun Tzu's admonitions on foreknowledge and spycraft indicate that Chinese generals during the Warring States period recognized the significant advantage of information superiority.[2] Intelligence is the second-oldest profession, quipped one author.[3]

Despite the timeless relationship between intelligence and war, much of the literature overlooks operational intelligence. Related scholarship focuses mainly on strategic or tactical intelligence and lacks sufficient depth of field to clearly depict intelligence at the operational level of war. This chapter aims to help fill that void.

Operational intelligence is, fundamentally, intelligence at the operational level of war.[4] This chapter analyzes and synthesizes these two constituent parts—intelligence and war's operational level—before proposing a definition of operational intelligence. First, it assesses classic and contemporary definitions of intelligence. Next, it traces the emergence of the operational level of war and describes its characteristics. Finally, it examines and defines operational intelligence.

Intelligence

No consensus definition of the kind of intelligence that relates to security exists. One author noted, "Intelligence holds distinct meanings for different people."[5] The historian Walter Laqueur cautioned, "All attempts to develop ambitious theories of intelligence have failed."[6] With these warnings in mind, we proceed judiciously toward a functional definition of intelligence.

Some scholars claim that "intelligence is information."[7] While valid, this definition is incomplete. Intelligence is a subset of information and something qualitatively different. First, not all information is intelligence.[8] Carl von Clausewitz, for example, referred to a specific kind of information: "By 'intelligence' we mean every sort of information about the enemy and his country."[9] Clausewitz provided context by placing intelligence in the same discourse as politics, war, and strategy. He also narrowed our concern to the adversary and the potential battlespace. Intelligence is information of a specific kind, but it is also far more.[10]

What, then, is intelligence? Sherman Kent, perhaps the preeminent American intelligence expert, identified three aspects of intelligence: knowledge, activity, and organization.[11] Summarizing Kent, one author wrote, "[Intelligence is] a particular kind of knowledge, the type of organization producing this knowledge, and the activity pursued by the organization."[12] Such knowledge encompasses more than the mere possession of data and is the result of concerted bureaucratic processes. Most subsequent scholarship either explicitly or implicitly incorporates Kent's framework.

Recent research on intelligence offers more descriptive definitions. For example, Mark Lowenthal contended that intelligence is "the process by which specific types of information important to national security are requested, collected, analyzed, and provided to policy makers; the products of that process; the safe-guarding of these processes and this information by counterintelligence activities; and the carrying out of operations as requested by lawful authorities."[13] Lowenthal's definition provides depth and breadth, and he adds helpful detail to the process. However, the expansion is unnecessary on two accounts. First, although crucial, counterintelligence is an ancillary function. Second, the catchall phrase regarding lawful operations—an allusion to covert action—distracts from the meaning of intelligence. It implies that intelligence is what intelligence organizations do, which is both tautological and unsatisfying. A final critique—Lowenthal's identification of policy makers as the singular set of intelligence consumers reveals his particular focus on the highest level of national security. Nonetheless, his emphasis on process and product is useful.

The US armed forces' definition of intelligence extends beyond the national level. Joint Publication (JP) 2-0 reads, "[Intelligence is the] product resulting from the collection, processing, integration, evaluation, analysis, and interpretation of available information concerning foreign nations, hostile or potentially hostile forces or elements, or areas of actual or potential operations. The term is also applied to the activity which results in the product and to the organizations engaged in such activity."[14] Careful readers will notice similarities between this definition and those from Clausewitz (potential adversaries and battlespace), Kent (knowledge, activity, organization), and Lowenthal (disaggregated process and resultant product). In contrast to Lowenthal, JP 2-0 does not limit the consumption of intelligence to policy makers, nor does it mention counterintelligence or covert action.

While detailed definitions can be instructive, they are also often unwieldy. Alternatively, Michael Warner reduced the concept to "secret, state activity to understand or influence foreign entities."[15] Warner's elegant offering moves us closer to the goal. Intelligence that is "performed by officers of the state for state purposes" warrants its official sanction.[16] Its core function is to understand. And identifying the subject of attention as foreign entities distinguishes intelligence from law enforcement or other domestic security activities. The term *foreign entities* is less restrictive than Clausewitz's concentration on the enemy. However, the breadth of Warner's definition, like that of Lowenthal's, suggests that he sought to encompass all Central Intelligence Agency (CIA) activities as much as he aimed to distill the essence of intelligence.

Three modifications to Warner's definition refine the concept. First, we can remove the adjective *secret*. Warner argued that "secrecy is the key to the definition of intelligence" and concluded that conceptualizing intelligence as clandestine distinguishes it from "other intellectual activities."[17] His point has merit but is overly restrictive. Much intelligence is collected overtly; limiting it to the secret realm risks excluding lucrative and inseparable surveillance, reconnaissance, and open-source collection activities.[18] Furthermore, the imperative to share intelligence coupled with the proliferation of coalition operations sometimes places traditional intelligence activities and products outside the formerly rigid lines of secrecy. Because intelligence is a state activity, the process and product very well may be kept secret. Then again, they may not.

The second adjustment to Warner's definition involves omitting the verb "to influence." Its inclusion confuses intelligence with activities designed to shape the outcome of events directly. Not every activity performed by an intelligence organization constitutes intelligence.[19] Expedience may place targeted killings, sabotage, or psychological operations within the purview of an intelligence agency.[20] However, these missions lie outside the central function of intelligence—to understand.

The Warner definition's third shortcoming is its omission of the spatial element. As previously noted, Clausewitz valued knowing the geography of potential battlegrounds. Modern warfare similarly benefits from awareness of the operational environment. Both entities and spaces are viable intelligence targets.

The purpose of intelligence is the final piece missing from our definition. Robert Bowie, a former Harvard professor who served as assistant secretary of state for policy planning and in the CIA, proposed that intelligence was "knowledge and analysis designed to assist action."[21] R. V. Jones concurred with Bowie when he wrote, "The ultimate object of intelligence is to enable action to be optimized."[22] Similarly, the prominent intelligence historian David Kahn concluded that the purpose of intelligence was to enable the efficient use of resources. [23] The use of resources is a function of the action to be taken; the nature of the action depends on circumstance, including the customer of the intelligence.

Thus, a refinement of the above contributions produces the following working definition: Intelligence is state activity to understand foreign entities and potential battlespaces for the purpose of informing action.[24]

The Operational Level of War

Understanding operational intelligence requires a brief description of the operational level of war. The intermediate perspective of military activity between the strategic and the tactical appeared with the massive expansion of armies brought about by the French Revolutionary *levée en masse* and the industrial revolution.[25] Previously, sovereigns accompanied their forces in limited conflicts, personally guiding the employment of force toward political objectives.[26] The nationalization and industrialization of war distanced policy makers from the battlefield and increasingly shifted the burden of connecting politics, strategy, and tactics to the soldier.[27]

The operational level of war is relatively new to American military discourse.[28] Some scholars trace the early emergence of the trifold stratification of war to Clausewitz's war plans, strategy, and tactics.[29] Baron Antoine-Henri Jomini identified six branches of Napoleonic war, including strategy, grand tactics, and minor tactics.[30] By the end of the nineteenth century, the German general Sigismund von Schlichting was among the first to recognize the emergence of operational art from industrial-age warfare.[31] In the 1930s, Soviet marshal Mikhail Tukhachevsky more fully developed the operational level with his "deep battle" concept and "deep operation theory."[32] Meanwhile, Anglo-American military thinkers overlooked this middle level of war. For example, the British strategic thinker Sir B. H. Liddell Hart set grand strategy above strategy and strategy directly above tactics without distinguishing the operational realm.[33] Post–World War II American strategists found little need for operational art in an era of material superiority and nuclear arms. Thus, the operational level of war—what Edward Luttwak called "the level that is most salient in the modern tradition of military thought in continental Europe"—remained absent from American military doctrine until the 1980s.[34]

Today, the operational level of war figures prominently in American military thought. JP 3-0 defines the levels of war as:

> Strategic Level—That level at which a nation, often as a member of a group, determines national or multinational (alliance or coalition) strategic security objectives and guidance and develops and uses national resources to accomplish these objectives.
>
> Operational Level—That level which links the tactical employment of forces to strategic objectives. The focus at this level is the operational art—the use of military forces to achieve strategic goals through the design, organization, integration, and conduct of strategies, campaigns, major operations, and battles. Operational art determines when, where, and for what purpose major forces will be employed.
>
> Tactical Level—Tactics is the employment of units in combat. It includes the ordered arrangement and maneuver of units in relation to each other and/or to the adversary in order to use their full potential. An engagement is normally short in duration and fought between small forces.[35]

Several characteristics distinguish the operational level.

1. It is removed from the political agency that resides at the level of strategy.
2. It is distinct from the actual employment of forces, which occurs at the tactical level.
3. It extends spatially beyond the tactical engagement but is less than global, often stopping before the international boundaries that demark the strategic.
4. It is sandwiched between the immediate and the enduring.

The operational level is also distinctly military although nonmilitary factors are not irrelevant (politics, economics, demographics, etc.). Almost by definition there is a significant martial characteristic to this level of war. In regular war, politics (national and international) and the coordination of nonmilitary instruments occur primarily in the strategic realm, which constitutes the upper bound of the operational level. In irregular war such coordination may be less distinguishable from operational-level military activities.

Finally, at its most abstract, the operational stratum is connective. It exists between and links together tactical effects and the strategic purpose, overlapping with and assuming characteristics of both. This linkage stretches operational commanders across all three levels of war. Commanders must be familiar with the particular dynamics of their intermediate perspective. However, in addition to participating in the development of military strategy and planning, they must guide battles and advise the formulation of policy and national strategy. Commanders at the operational level must be equally comfortable with the tactical and strategic. Consequently, so must their intelligence.

Operational Intelligence

Gradual appreciation of a distinct category of operational intelligence followed the emergence of an operational level of war. Previously, as Dennis Showalter explored in his analysis of intelligence prior to World War I, operational intelligence meant "securing knowledge of the movements, capacities and intentions of other armed forces" and was indivisible from the skillful scouting performed by light cavalry units.[36] Operational intelligence was tactical reconnaissance writ large.[37]

This conception of operational intelligence slowly expanded over time. American doctrine now trifurcates intelligence in conjunction with the levels of war:

> Strategic intelligence—Intelligence required for the formation of policy and military plans at national and international levels.
>
> Operational intelligence—Intelligence required for planning and conducting campaigns and major operations to accomplish strategic objectives within theaters or operational areas.
>
> Tactical intelligence—Intelligence required for the planning and conduct of tactical operations.[38]

However, not all scholarship recognizes or accurately depicts the intermediate level. Much of the literature still divides intelligence into the tactical and strategic. Melanie Gutjahr provides one example:

> Generally, intelligence has been placed into two categories—tactical and strategic. This delineation was driven primarily by the principal consumer—military commanders or policymakers. Operational (tactical) intelligence is knowledge about the immediate situation and is based almost entirely on straightforward observation. Strategic intelligence has a wider base and broader objective, integrating economics, politics, social studies, and the study of technology. Strategic intelligence provides policymakers with the "big picture" whereas tactical intelligence provides the "front yard" view. The main difference between strategic and tactical warning is the time horizon.[39]

This passage depicts strategic and tactical intelligence with some accuracy. Strategic intelligence, like the strategic level of war, is "big picture" and dominated by the policy maker. It is, as Kent explained, "the knowledge upon which we base our high-level national policy toward the other states of the world."[40] Meanwhile, tactical intelligence exists in the realm of combat force employment. In their book on ancient Roman intelligence, N. J. R. Austin and

N. E. Rankov described tactical intelligence as addressing "the immediate problem of how to find the enemy and face them in operations once hostilities have broken out."[41] However, by overlooking the operational level of war, Gutjahr and others conflate operational and tactical intelligence. Tactical intelligence is near, immediate, and straightforward; practitioners know operational intelligence cannot be so limited.

Michael Handel described operational intelligence as "intelligence in war and military operations."[42] Clausewitz, who wrote extensively on what we label the operational level of war, called intelligence "the basis, in short, of our plans and operations."[43] Operational intelligence informs the military commander's alignment of tactical employment with strategic objectives in a given area and facilitates the conduct of subsequent operations.[44] Within its purview is all that relates to the commander's mission and area of responsibility: the near and far, the immediate and future, the tactical and strategic. Perhaps then-major Ronald Burgess captured it best when he wrote, "Operational intelligence is more or less the fusion of tactical and strategic intelligence to respond to operational requirements."[45]

Finally, operational intelligence, like the operational level of war, has a distinctive military character. However, operational intelligence is not synonymous with military intelligence for two reasons. First, military intelligence may exist at the strategic, operational, or tactical levels of war. Operational intelligence is, by definition, intelligence at the operational level of war. Second, depending on the conflict's circumstances, operational intelligence may not be restricted to military sources or the analysis of military professionals. Increasingly, and most evidently in irregular war, military and nonmilitary intelligence entities collaborate on challenges at all levels of war. Thus, operational intelligence is not limited to military activity.

Conclusions

Building on the earlier definition of intelligence, operational intelligence is state activity to understand foreign entities and potential battlespaces for the purpose of planning and conducting campaigns and major operations; perforce, it must also include some consideration of strategy and tactics. The quest for understanding is elusive, especially in war.

Notes

1. Van Creveld, *Command in War*, 264.
2. Num. 13:1 and Josh. 2:1; and Sun Tzu, *Illustrated Art of War*, 103, 125, 231–39.

3. Knightley, *Second Oldest Profession*, 3.

4. Gray, *Explorations in Strategy*, 61; and Kelly and Brennan, *Alien*, 7–8. I find the levels of war a rigid and hierarchical framework that, when applied to reality, becomes inadequate quickly. I prefer a more abstract distinction between tactics and strategy provided by Gray when he wrote, "Namely, whereas tactics is the realm of the actual employment of armed forces, strategy refers to the intended or real consequences of the use of forces for the course and outcome of a war." Between strategy and tactics exists the operational art which Kelly and Brennan described as "a continuous conversation between strategic ends, i.e., that which is to be achieved; and tactical means, i.e., that which is to be done." At which level of the state and military bureaucracy strategy and operational art occur depends on the circumstance. Similarly, context determines the scope and richness of the operational art. However, because the levels-of-war construct is more straightforward and well known, it offers a useful device for conceptualizing the intermediary realm between strategy and tactics and allows this project to proceed. The levels of war, therefore, serve the purpose of this project.

5. Gutjahr, *Intelligence Archipelago*, 7.

6. Laqueur, *A World of Secrets*, 8.

7. Berkowitz and Goodman, *Best Truth*, x.

8. Lowenthal, *Intelligence*, 1.

9. Clausewitz, *On War*, 117.

10. Warner, "Wanted," 17.

11. Kent, *Strategic Intelligence*, xxv.

12. Herman, *Intelligence Services*, 3.

13. Lowenthal, *Intelligence*, 8.

14. JP 2-0, *Joint Intelligence*, GL-11.

15. Warner, "Wanted," 19.

16. Ibid.

17. Ibid., 18, quoting Shulsky, *Silent Warfare*, 1–3.

18. Kent, *Strategic Intelligence*, 152; and Deptula and Brown, "A House Divided," 5–15.

19. Executive Order (EO) 12333, para. 3.5(g). Admittedly, EO12333 seemingly contradicts this assertion by defining intelligence activities as "all activities that agencies within the intelligence community are authorized to conduct pursuant to this Order." However, this author contends that there remains a difference between intelligence and the overarching and legally necessary term *intelligence activities*.

20. Powers, *Intelligence Wars*; Turner, *Burn before Reading*; Dulles, *Craft of Intelligence*; and Hunt, *American Spy*. These fascinating unclassified histories of the CIA were useful.

21. May, *Knowing One's Enemies*, 3.

22. Jones, "Intelligence and Command," 288.

23. Kahn, "An Historical Theory," 8.

24. The author prefers the domain-neutral term *space* because it accommodates all potential "fields" of battle.

25. Kelly and Brennan, *Alien*, 11.

26. Ibid.

27. Ibid., 12.

28. Simpkin, *Deep Battle*, x.

29. Winton, "Strategy, Operational Art"; and Clausewitz, *On War*, 128, 177, 358, and 577. Winton observed how Clausewitz's understanding of strategy aligns with contemporary concepts of operational art.

30. Jomini, *Art of War*, 11.

31. Cranz, "Understanding Change," 10.

32. Simpkin, *Deep Battle*, x–xi, 35.

33. Hart, *Strategy*, 321–23.

34. Luttwak, "Operational Level of War," 61.

35. JP 3-0, *Joint Doctrine for Operations*, II-2-3.

36. Showalter, "Intelligence on the Eve," 16–17; and Deptula and Brown, "A House Divided," 5–15.

37. Showalter, "Intelligence on the Eve," 17.

38. JP 2-0, *Joint Intelligence*, GL-15–16.

39. Gutjahr, *Intelligence Archipelago*, 8. In making her argument, Gutjahr cites Bruce D. Berkowitz and Allan E. Goodman, *Strategic Intelligence for American Security* (Princeton, NJ: Princeton University Press, 1989), 4. I take exception only with Gutjahr's characterization of operational intelligence and find many aspects of her project's assessment of intelligence reform useful.

40. Kent, *Strategic Intelligence*, 3.

41. Austin and Rankov, *Exploratio*, 39.

42. Handel, *Intelligence and Military Operations*, 1.

43. Clausewitz, *On War*, 117.

44. MacLachlan, *Intelligence*, 53–54; and Jones, "Intelligence and Command," 288.

45. Burgess, "Operational Intelligence," 8.

Chapter 3

The Practice of Operational Intelligence

Therefore I say: "Know the enemy and know yourself; in a hundred battles you will never be in peril. When you are ignorant of the enemy but know yourself, your chances of winning or losing are equal. If ignorant both of your enemy and yourself, you are certain in every battle to be in peril."

—Sun Tzu
The Art of War

Finally, the general unreliability of all information presents a special problem in war: all action takes place, so to speak, in a kind of twilight, which like fog or moonlight, often tends to make things seem grotesque and larger than they really are.

—Carl von Clausewitz
On War

The effective practice of operational intelligence is a complicated endeavor upon which military success frequently hinges. Accomplishing Sun Tzu's imperative to understand the enemy and oneself is seldom straightforward.[1] Everything in war is difficult, including intelligence.[2] Carl von Clausewitz observed that the frictions of war obscure visibility in it as a fog distorts reality.[3] Sun Tzu acknowledged the complexity of war when he wrote, "Now in war there may be one hundred changes in each step."[4] Discerning the intent, or even actions, of an uncooperative foe requires great skill, effort, and often luck.

Because clarity in war is so difficult, the side that achieves it relative to the other garners a distinct advantage. Many accounts of intelligence-enabled success in combat exist.[5] Even intelligence failures—surprises—underscore how crucial understanding is in war.[6] It can arguably be decisive.[7] So how is such advantage pursued?

This chapter examines the practice of operational intelligence using its most essential elements. It begins by sketching the purposes, consumers, processes, and products of operational intelligence. It then considers the two most central functions of intelligence operations—collection and analysis. The chapter concludes that the acquisition of information and its transduction into knowledge are the basic activities of intelligence that support subordinate elements, planners, and commanders.

Deconstructing Operational Intelligence

The previous chapter concluded that operational intelligence is state activity to understand foreign entities and potential battlespaces for the purpose of planning and conducting campaigns and major operations; perforce, it must also include some consideration of strategy and tactics. The purposes, consumers, products, and processes of operational intelligence derive from this definition.

The ultimate purpose of intelligence is to optimize resources and action.[8] It does so by informing strategies, campaigns, operations, and battles. Joint doctrine elaborates: "The purposes of joint intelligence that guide the intelligence directorate of a joint staff (J-2) and those of supporting organizations are: inform the commander; identify, define, and nominate objectives; support the planning and execution of operations; counter adversary deception and surprise; support friendly deception efforts; and assess the effects of operations on the adversary."[9]

Three consumers emerge from this description: the commander, the planner, and subordinate elements. Each is important; however, the commander—the key military decision maker—is crucial. Commanders drive planning and execution. According to Michael Handel, intelligence supports the commander by supplying the information necessary to reach a decision, then assessing the outcome of that decision.[10] Commanders and directors of intelligence together develop priority intelligence requirements (PIR), the questions that guide subsequent collection and analytical efforts.[11] Strategic and operational-level assessments focus on the command's overall effectiveness in accomplishing high-level and intermediate objectives, while tactical assessments scrutinize performance measures.[12]

Intelligence support to planning occurs throughout the planning process. The development of concepts and plans relies on timely information and robust analytical estimates that assess the operational environment, adversary capabilities, and enemy courses of action. The intelligence officer concurrently develops an intelligence concept of operations and plan to support the successful execution of the commander's overarching plan.[13] Furthermore, as the plan is executed, continual assessments help refine subsequent planning and identify previously unforeseen opportunities and vulnerabilities.

JP 2-0 asserts, "Intelligence support is crucial to all aspects of execution."[14] Execution is a wide-ranging activity that includes mobilization, deployment, employment, sustainment, redeployment, and demobilization efforts throughout all phases of operations.[15] Facilitating the action of subordinate elements is multifaceted, demanding significant resources.

For example, because operational commanders often retain targeting approval authority, their intelligence officers control the otherwise tactical discipline of target intelligence. The heavy volume of requirements generated during the execution of operations stresses most intelligence organizations. Consequently, intelligence officers spend significant energy orchestrating persistent and dynamic sensors to enable shared situational awareness (current intelligence) and target development (target intelligence) for tactical forces executing their missions.

Intelligence also supports the commander during an operation's execution. According to JP 2-01, "Commanders use intelligence to anticipate the battle, visualize and understand the full spectrum battlespace, and influence the outcome of operations."[16]

The various responsibilities of operational intelligence require products in the form of advice, estimates, assessments, and plans.[17] JP 2-0 categorizes these by their purpose: indications and warning (I&W), current, general military, target, scientific and technical, counterintelligence, and estimative intelligence.[18] Generally, longer-term estimates support commanders and planners, while more immediate awareness and targeting intelligence services subordinate elements. However, product relevance for each consumer varies with circumstance.

Directors of intelligence employ a functional process to provide consumers required support and products. Intelligence professionals learn the six interrelated categories of the intelligence operations model: planning and direction, collection, processing and exploitation, analysis and production, dissemination and integration, and evaluation and feedback.[19] Each stage is vital, but two activities comprise the bulk of intelligence operations—collection and analysis.[20]

Collection: Illuminating the Battlespace

Collection is, arguably, the main activity of intelligence.[21] It is the sensing of the surrounding world, the figurative act of peering into fog-enshrouded battlespace. Sherman Kent called collection "the surveillance operation" by which something or someplace "is put under close and systematic observation."[22] It is the surveillance and reconnaissance portion of the contemporary acronym ISR (intelligence, surveillance, and reconnaissance).[23] Collection is, in essence, the acquisition of information.

Collection systems offer obvious military advantages. Ancient armies employed agents, deployed scouts, and intercepted messages in their quest for understanding.[24] Military services still do. As man took to the air, and later space, so did their intelligence sensors.[25] Information-age systems of systems now provide significant battlespace awareness; for some techno-optimists, perfect knowledge is inevitable.[26] Until then, intelligence professionals must balance information requirements with available collection assets.

Collection managers aim to acquire data that implements their collection plan.[27] That plan aggregates requirements from various consumers—the commander, planners, and tactical forces. PIRs, the intelligence subset of the commander's critical information requirements, articulate questions commanders and planners ask about the enemy and operational environment.[28] PIRs are products of operational decision-making and planning processes, typically linked directly to decision points identified in the plan.[29] Additionally, subordinate forces submit collection requirements to facilitate tactical planning and execution.[30]

A variety of sensors are available for collection activities, depending on resources and circumstance. JP 2-0 categorizes collection means into the categories of human, geospatial (imagery and cartography), signals, (communications, electronic, etc.), measurement and signature, open-source, and technical intelligence.[31] As well, so-called nontraditional ISR assets may be available to perform surveillance or reconnaissance tasks similar to scouts throughout history. Understanding the relative merits of each sensor is the duty of professionals who seek to optimize the use of collection resources.

Collection managers at the operational level must also consider which capabilities are available for direct employment and which remain controlled at higher or lower levels of command.[32] It is a peculiar characteristic of the American operational-level joint command that it may control few intelligence collection assets directly. Requirements for collection using national-level capabilities are prioritized within the combatant commander's headquarters before adjudication at the national level.[33] Conversely, because service doctrine shapes the presentation of component forces to the joint commander, lower-echelon commanders may retain control over the majority of ISR assets.[34] The Joint Collection Management Board manages those collection assets made available for operational-level taskings.

Prior to and during combat operations, intelligence directors oversee the competition for limited collection assets. Constant tension exists between satisfying the campaign requirements and facilitating the operations of subordinate elements. Collection managers prioritize requirements and match the optimal sensors with the essential elements of information derived from each requirement.[35] This ordering manifests itself on the joint integrated prioritized collection list.

Intelligence collection strives to reduce uncertainty by illuminating the battlespace. However, collection is only one intelligence activity. Converting observations into knowledge is the enterprise of analysis. For intelligence to function effectively, collection and analysis must be tightly coupled.[36]

Analysis: Thinking through the Fog

Analysis develops knowledge from collected information.[37] It is the "thinking part of the intelligence process."[38] Kent referred to it as research, which he argued was the attempt to ascertain meaningful patterns from past and present observations.[39] Joint doctrine calls it the process by which intelligence is produced.[40] While collection often comprises the majority of effort, the analytical function is most central to intelligence. As one scholar averred, "Analysts and analysts alone create intelligence."[41]

Like collection, analysis is as old as war. The limited scale of ancient warfare made the commander's intuition sufficient to his or her analytical needs.[42] As the size of armies and warfare increased, analytical requirements outgrew the capacity of a single mind.[43] Permanent organizations of specialized analysts developed at every level of command. By the end of World War II, Sir Harry Hinsley reflected, "Intelligence [was] unlikely ever again to return to the age of innocence—to that condition of general neglect interspersed with bursts of belated and amateur endeavor in times of crisis."[44] Commanders must still think for themselves, but they also rely on expert analysts to aid their understanding of the enemy and the operational environment.

Analysts at the operational level of war support commanders, planners, and lower-echelon forces. Regarding the latter, facilitating tactical action is straightforward and immediate; that is, is there a tank on the other side of this hill? Answers are precise. These questions are numerous in war but typically demand little analytical depth. On rare occasions, such as the search for high-value targets, analysis to facilitate the employment of forces requires significant resources.[45] As a rule, however, analytical support to commanders and planners is more complicated than the support given to tactical forces. Theirs are the questions of knowledge on which strategies and campaigns hang.

How intelligence generates knowledge is a question of epistemology.[46] James Bruce identified five principal ways of knowing: reference to authority, habit of thought or conventional wisdom, rationalism, empiricism, and science. Kent called this process "the instruments of reason and the scientific method" applied by a thoughtful individual.[47] Karl Popper famously argued that scientific learning occurs through the refutation of hypotheses.[48] Because few things can be proven, scientists must ask the questions that can disprove a proposition. Richards J. Heuer Jr. averred that rationalism, specifically deductive reasoning, dominates the practice of intelligence.[49] Thus, analysis is clearly a cognitive process.

By definition, analysis is reductive, breaking complex subjects into smaller parts to gain understanding. To become aware of adversaries and potential battlespaces requires consideration of numerous objective and subjective factors.[50] The former are measurable—for example, geography, climate, demographics, gross domestic product, lines of communication, location of forces, and so forth. While objective factors may present a collection challenge, they usually call for straightforward analytical efforts. In contrast, subjective factors—such as commander's intent, force capability, population resiliency, system recuperability, cultural disposition, and so forth—are less tangible. Analyzing combinations of objective and subjective factors is the specialized, cognitive craft of intelligence professionals.

However, reductionism alone is insufficient for understanding the interconnected battlespace. Ernest May referred to intelligence assessments as comparisons of capability that take the proclivities of an opponent into account.[51] Analysis of an adversary's capability and proclivity at the operational level of war must account for the innumerable links that exist among combinations of objective and subjective factors. Analysis must account for systems.

Peter Checkland defined a system as "the idea of a set of elements connected together which form a whole . . . [with] properties which are properties of the whole, rather than properties of its component parts."[52] For example, more complete understanding of the enemy and battlespace occurs when the characteristics of a specific air defense missile battery become a subset of knowledge about the integrated air and missile defense system (IADS), when the IADS is recognized as part of a military command and control system, when the military is seen within the context of a larger political system that is interrelated with an economic system, and when politics and economics are placed inside a larger social system. Analytical knowledge comes from understanding the relationships within and between relevant systems.

Additionally, juxtaposing the commander's strategic goals with a systems understanding of the opponent and battlespace informs the critical factor analysis that identifies adversary center(s) of gravity and critical capabilities, requirements, and vulnerabilities.[53] Matching what is to be achieved with a systems understanding of the adversary and operational environment provides insight into potentially feasible operational concepts. It also permits analysts to consider the possible effects of action. American joint doctrine calls its systematic and continuous analytical approach to understanding rel-

24

evant systems and their relation to strategic goals the joint intelligence preparation of the operational environment (JIPOE).[54]

Like all cognition, analysis is subject to pathologies of the mind. Analysts
develop implicit mental models—paradigms and schema—based on con-
scious and unconscious assumptions used to manage complexity, uncertainty,
and information overload.[55] An analyst's degree of cultural awareness about
the subject may affect the model.[56] Structural factors also shape analytical
models. For example, Richard Betts wrote, "Policy premises constrict perception, and administrative workloads constrain reflection."[57] Models can be useful, but they can also be inaccurate. Heuer concluded, "Accurate estimates
depend as much on the mental model used in forming the picture as upon the
number of pieces of the puzzle that have been collected."[58] Analysts often perceive what they expect to perceive.[59]

Heuristic patterns are resistant to change. Analysts need cognitive closure
to establish answers upon which subsequent analysis can build.[60] At the macro
level, closure is manifested in the termination of discourse regarding an issue.[61] An innate desire for clarity deters thinkers—analysts and decision makers alike—from reexamining a model's assumptions.[62] Deficiencies in logic
are unavoidable, resistant to modification, and a threat to accurate and reliable intelligence.[63]

Cognitive biases require rigorous countermeasures. Heuer offered several,
including constructing methodical hypotheses, competing hypotheses, and
comparing historical analogies.[64] Betts presented the most fundamental advice for addressing analytical pathologies by suggesting that we recognize the
inherent shortcomings of analysis, consciously think about thinking, and develop a tolerance for disaster.[65] Accurate analysis requires critical thinking,
but critical thinking is not a guarantor of accuracy.[66]

Analysis is not fortune telling.[67] It cannot predict the future, only estimate it.
Complicated problems—those with many interconnected objective and subjective factors—are inherently unpredictable. Thus, estimates are exercises in
probability. Clausewitz provided the following insight on estimates at the operational level of war: "From the enemy's character, from his institutions, the
state of his affairs, and his general situation, each side, using the laws of probability, forms an estimate of its opponent's likely course and acts accordingly."[68]

According to Betts, because analysis is inherently inaccurate in predicting
the future, so-called intelligence failures are "not only inevitable, they are natural."[69] However, the term's use often indicates an ignorance of intelligence by
the speaker. As Betts explained, "In the best known cases of intelligence failure, the most crucial mistakes have seldom been made by collectors of raw
information, occasionally by professionals who produce finished analyses,

but most often by the decision makers who consume the products of intelligence services."[70] The questions and assumptions that drive analysis are those of the decision maker. At the operational level of war, as at all other levels, this burden rests with the commander.

To refine this point, an appreciation of the limits of analysis is crucial to fully exploiting the potential of intelligence. May contended, "A better test [of merit] than accuracy or acceptability may be simply whether assessments address the right questions: that is, the questions right answers to which could be useful guides to action."[71] Analysts at the operational level of war are limited by their resources, especially time and the priorities they are given. Unless otherwise directed, those priorities—those questions—are the commander's PIRs.

Commanders comfortable with intelligence at the operational level of war are more tolerant of its imprecision relative to tactical intelligence. Joseph Nye described analysts as educators: "Rather than trying to predict the future, estimators should deal with heightened uncertainty by presenting alternative scenarios. To be useful, estimates must describe not only the nature and probability of the most likely future paths, but they must also investigate significant excursions off those paths and identify signposts that would tell us we are entering such territory."[72] Alternative scenarios are like alternate hypotheses, the pursuit of which requires a willingness to accept cognitive dissonance. This can be discomforting to a commander who is invested in a particular operational approach. Furthermore, commanders must want to be educated.

As with collection operations, intelligence directors must balance their support of the commander and staff with analytical support to tactical forces. This is no easy challenge as both pull from finite intelligence resources. Andrew Marshall, the director of the Office of Net Assessment, cautioned that collection and analysis of one type of assessment could impair another.[73] Previously, I asserted that the commander was the most important consumer of operational intelligence. However, when commanders disengage from their intelligence process, other forces can influence the balance of analysis. The questions that underpin strategies and campaigns are ambiguous and the analysis inconclusive. In contrast, the questions that facilitate tactical action are often tangible, answerable, and gratifying. There is a natural tendency for analysis at the operational level to gravitate toward the latter given the demands of limited resources, time, and the imperative of action.

A final point on analysis at the operational level of war regards the importance of linking analytical resources and aggregating information. Analytical requirements inevitably exceed the capacity of collection assets. Not all collection capabilities are available to the joint force commander for employment; regardless, the appetite for intelligence is insatiable. Nevertheless, important information is often collected by ISR platforms organic to tactical forces or by the forces themselves. Finding and funneling this information from tactical units to the operational-level analytical centers can greatly improve the shared understanding of the joint force.[74] Directors of intelligence must build networks of analysts to share information and expertise effectively.

Conclusions

Sun Tzu admonished us to understand the enemy. The practice of intelligence involves the collection of information about the adversary and the fog-covered battlespace and the analysis of that data to produce knowledge. The Chinese theorist also advised us to understand ourselves. Successful analysis requires critical thinking, including an awareness of cognitive biases and the limitations of intelligence. Collection and analysis are the two primary functions operational intelligence performs to support subordinate forces, planners, and commanders. Directors of intelligence must balance their support among these customers. While support to tactical forces facilitates action, the operational-level commander shapes the strategy and owns the campaign. Systems analyses, like that in the JIPOE, help build a realistic understanding of the adversary and the battlespace, supporting plan development and the operational-level commander's decision-making process. Ultimately, intelligence outputs—advice, estimates, and assessments—must support the commander. After all, intelligence professionals are an extension of the commander's mind.

Notes

1. Sun Tzu, *Illustrated Art of War*, 125.
2. Clausewitz, *On War*, 119.
3. Ibid., 140.
4. Sun Tzu, *Illustrated Art of War*, 124.
5. Several useful accounts of intelligence-enabled success are recorded in Kahn, *The Codebreakers*; Hitchcock, "Intelligence Revolution"; Handel, *Leaders and Intelligence*; Handel, *Intelligence and Military Operations*; Norwitz, "Leveraging Operational Intelligence"; and Elder, "Intelligence in War."
6. Elder, "Intelligence in War," makes this point decisively. For examples of intelligence shortfalls, see Hughes-Wilson, *Military Intelligence Blunders*; Keegan, *Intelligence in War*; and Dyson, "A Failure of Intelligence."
7. Elder, "Intelligence in War."
8. Kahn, "An Historical Theory," 8; and Jones, "Intelligence and Command," 288.
9. JP 2-0, *Joint Intelligence*, ix.

10. Handel, *Leadership and Intelligence*, 9.

11. JP 2-0, *Joint Intelligence*, I-8, IV-6.

12. Ibid., IV-19–24.

13. Ibid., IV-7–9.

14. Ibid., IV-10.

15. Ibid., IV-10–11.

16. JP 2-01, *Joint and National Intelligence Support*, xi.

17. For a list of J-2 responsibilities, see JP 2-0, *Joint Intelligence*, III-15.

18. Ibid., I-16.

19. Ibid., I-7.

20. Kent, *Strategic Intelligence*, 4; Betts, "Analysis, War, and Decision," 61; and Herman, *Intelligence Services*, 4.

21. Herman, *Intelligence Services*, 4.

22. Kent, *Strategic Intelligence*, 4.

23. Deptula and Brown, "A House Divided," 5–7.

24. For some ancient examples of military intelligence, see Herodotus, *Histories*, 315–16; Thucydides, *Landmark Thucydides*, 58–59; Austin and Rankov, *Exploratio*, 246; Arquilla and Ronfeldt, "Cyberwar Is Coming," 152–55; and Kahn, *Codebreakers*, 71–80.

25. For accounts of early air- and space-borne intelligence collection, see Jomini, *Art of War*, 251; Maslowski, "Military Intelligence Sources," 50; Kennett, *First Air War*, 7, 18; Ruffner, *CORONA*; and Norris, *Spies in the Sky*.

26. Owens, "Emerging System of Systems," 15; and Libicki, "DBK and Its Consequences," 28.

27. JP 2-0, *Joint Intelligence*, I-14.

28. Ibid., I-8.

29. JP 2-01, *Joint and National Intelligence Support*, II-2; and Spinuzzi, "CCIR for Complex and Uncertain Environments," 18–22.

30. JP 2-0, *Joint Intelligence*, I-10.

31. Ibid., I-6.

32. JP 2-01, *Joint and National Intelligence Support*, III-13.

33. Collection management responsibility for worldwide military requirements of national-level assets rests with the Defense Intelligence Operations Coordination Center (DIOCC) at the Defense Intelligence Agency. The DIOCC advocates military requirements within the intelligence community.

34. The advantages and disadvantages of each service's philosophy on the control of ISR assets are beyond the scope of this paper. The necessary point is that joint directors of intelligence, on behalf of the joint commanders, must manipulate various levers to task and synchronize the collection of intelligence requirements. For more on the individual service doctrines, see discussion on intelligence in the modular force in Field Manual (FM) 2-0, *Intelligence*, 2–6. Navy doctrine similarly conceptualizes the employment of intelligence assets as organic capabilities that facilitate maritime operations; however, it does refer to both "top down and bottom up intelligence support." Naval Doctrine Publication 2, *Naval Intelligence*, 38. Air Force doctrine explicitly broaches the collection operations management control by joint authorities of air component ISR assets in Air Force Doctrine Document 2-9, *Intelligence, Surveillance, and Reconnaissance Operations*, 39–46.

35. JP 2-0, *Joint Intelligence*, I-9.

36. Bundy, "Guiding of Intelligence Collection," 37–53; Gazit, "Estimates and Fortune-Telling," 40–41; and Bruce, "Missing Link," 206. For more on feedback loops and system coupling, see Perrow, *Normal Accidents*, 62–100.

37. Mangio and Wilkinson, "Intelligence Analysis," 3.

38. Bruce and George, "Intelligence Analysis," 1.

39. Kent, *Strategic Intelligence*, 4.

40. JP 2-0, *Joint Intelligence*, I-15.

41. Moore, *Critical Thinking*, 1.

42. Thomas, "U.S. Military Intelligence Analysis," 138. For an explanation of how intuition is analyzed based on personal experience and judgment, see Gladwell, *Blink*. For examples and discussions on analysis by ancient commanders, see Exod. 17:8–13; Herodotus, *Histories*, 476–83; Caesar, *Caesar's Commentaries*, 7; Luvaas, "Napoleon's Use of Intelligence," 40–54; Rosello, "Clausewitz's Contempt for Intelligence," 11–20; and van Creveld, *Command in War*, 56–57.

43. Showalter, "Intelligence on the Eve," 18.

44. Hinsley, "World War II," 4.

45. Deptula, "Think Different."

46. Bruce, "Making Analysis More Reliable," 171.

47. Heuer, *Psychology of Intelligence Analysis*, xiv.

48. Popper, *Logic of Scientific Discovery*.

49. Heuer, *Psychology of Intelligence Analysis*, 59–60.

50. The importance of accurate analysis of objective and subjective conditions is discussed in the irregular warfare literature. Useful lists of factors that comprise the operational environment are in JP 2-01.3, *Joint Intelligence Preparation of the Operational Environment* and *US Army-Marine Corps Counterinsurgency Field Manual*, 82–113. Also see Kiras, "Irregular Warfare," 253; Guevara, *Guerilla Warfare*, 148–62; and Flynn, Pottinger, and Batchelor, *Fixing Intel*.

51. May, "Capabilities and Proclivities," 503.

52. Checkland, *Systems Thinking*, 3.

53. JP 2-01.3, *Joint Intelligence Preparation of the Operational Environment*, xviii–xxi.

54. Ibid., xi; and JP 2-0, *Joint Intelligence*, I-16.

55. Heuer, *Psychology of Intelligence Analysis*, 60. Also see Popper, *Open Society and Its Enemies*, 289; Kuhn, *Structure of Scientific Revolutions*; and Jervis, *Perception and Misperception*.

56. Porter, *Military Orientalism*, 13–19.

57. Betts, "Analysis, War, and Decision," 61.

58. Heuer, *Psychology of Intelligence Analysis*, 62.

59. Ibid., 8.

60. Hatlebrekke and Smith, "Towards a New Theory," 148–49. Also see Kruglanski, *Lay Epistemics and Human Knowledge*, 14; and Bar-Joseph, "Intelligence Failure," 182.

61. Hatlebrekke and Smith, "Towards a New Theory," 156–60.

62. Ibid., 149.

63. Heuer, *Psychology of Intelligence Analysis*, 11.

64. Ibid., 32–35, 38, 95–107. For additional techniques see Hall and Citrenbaum, *Intelligence Analysis*; and Heuer and Pherson, *Structured Analytic Techniques*.

65. Betts, "Analysis, War, and Decision," 83–89.

66. Moore, *Critical Thinking*, 8–12. Moore argued that the US intelligence community should institutionalize the elements of critical thinking as described by Elder and Paul, *Foundations of Analytic Thinking*.

67. Gazit, "Estimates and Fortune-Telling," 36–56; and Nye, "Peering into the Future," 82–93.

68. Clausewitz, *On War*, 80.

69. Betts, "Analysis, War, and Decision," 54.

70. Ibid., 61. For more on the literature of analytical surprise, see Chan, "Intelligence of Stupidity," 171–80; Gazit, "Estimates and Fortune-Telling"; Levite, *Intelligence and Strategic Surprises*; Betts, "Surprise, Scholasticism, and Strategy," 329–43; and Nye, "Peering into the Future."

71. May, "Capabilities and Proclivities," 504.

72. Nye, "Peering into the Future," 93.

73. May, "Capabilities and Proclivities," 5.

74. Flynn, Pottinger, and Batchelor, *Fixing Intel*, 9, 12–13.

Chapter 4

Operational Intelligence and the Commander

The necessity of procuring good intelligence is apparent and need not be further urged—all that remains for me to add, is that you keep the whole matter as secret as possible. For upon Secrecy, Success depends in most enterprises of the kind, and for want of it, they are generally defeated, however well planned and promising a favorable issue.

—George Washington

Many intelligence reports in war are contradictory; even more are false, and most are uncertain. What one can reasonably ask of an officer is that he should possess a standard of judgment, which he can gain only from knowledge of men and affairs and from common sense.

—Carl von Clausewitz
On War

For Carl von Clausewitz, the elusiveness of clarity in war elevated the importance of the commander's judgment.[1] His experiences made him skeptical about the utility of intelligence.[2] However, Clausewitz was as familiar with the failures of Prussian intelligence as he was ignorant of the successes of Napoleon Bonaparte's sophisticated intelligence system.[3] Intelligence in today's construct is a complicated process of collection and analysis about the enemy and battlespace on behalf of the commander. Intelligence informs the commander's judgment.

Early commanders performed many of their own intelligence activities. They sought high ground to survey the enemy and managed spy networks.[4] Past great commanders conducted intelligence analysis, synthesizing various fragments of collected information.[5] Such was the practice of intelligence through Clausewitz's time.

As war increased in scale and complexity, intelligence did likewise. Permanent intelligence staffs became common among European powers by the late nineteenth century, and reliance on individual coup d'oeil gave way to more systematic and wide-ranging methods.[6] At the height of World War II, tens of thousands of analysts, cartographers, photo interpreters, cryptologists, linguists, mathematicians, and engineers labored to reduce strategic and operational uncertainty.[7] Today, interconnected constellations of sensors networked with computer-aided intelligence professionals illuminate battlespaces with a degree of detail unknown to Clausewitz.[8] The contemporary practice of intelligence is more complicated than it was in the past, but its primary purpose remains unchanged. Operational intelligence supplements the commander's mind.

This chapter discusses the central role of the commander in the practice of operational intelligence. It identifies the commander's personality, experience, and self-perceptions of vulnerability and expertise as variables that shape the use of intelligence. Next, it outlines useful traits of key intelligence advisors as they relate to the commander, including rapport, integrity, courage, expertise, and communication skills. The chapter concludes that the single most important determinant of the success of operational intelligence is the commander. At the operational level of war, supple-minded commanders with experience digesting, assessing, and synthesizing intelligence are best positioned to lead intelligence operations and translate their insights into effective action.

Before beginning, it is necessary to comment on the chapter's research. The topic under consideration is the relationship between the commander and operational intelligence; therefore, the chapter prefers sources that concentrate on decision makers at the operational level of war. However, it does not ignore the substantial body of scholarship that scrutinizes multiple aspects of national-level decision making and the use of strategic intelligence.[9] Where it is appropriate, this chapter borrows insights and illustrations from the strategic-level literature and extends them to the operational level of war.

The Commander

The quality of the commander has significant bearing on the effectiveness of operational intelligence.[10] Ultimately, the commander is responsible for guiding intelligence system activities.[11] Michael Handel wrote, "Although there is no ideal type of leader for the optimal use of intelligence, personality and experience are extremely important."[12] Personality, experience, and self-perceptions of vulnerability and expertise affect a commander's ability to exploit operational intelligence.

Personality is a complex set of cognitive, attitudinal, and behavioral elements.[13] A substantial body of psychological research exists regarding some strategic-level decision makers. For example, Alexander and Juliette George found three aspects of personality particularly relevant to a leader's decision-making patterns.[14] The first was cognitive style, or "the way in which he defines informational needs . . . and his preferred ways of acquiring and utilizing information and advice from others."[15] Other personality facets important to decision making include the leader's sense of competence on the matter at hand and interpersonal relations.[16]

The personality extremes of Adolph Hitler and Winston Churchill illustrate the effect of personality on intelligence receptivity. According to David Jablonsky, Hitler's decision making was instinctive, compulsive, unremitting, and unitary.[17] Hitler's press chief described him as unteachable, and one of his general officers attributed to him an "almost wild-animal perception for anything which ran counter to himself."[18] These traits made Hitler extremely resistant to new or contrary information and incapable of fully exploiting intelligence when making decisions.[19] Churchill, by contrast, passionately embraced intelligence. Christopher Andrew ascribed the prime minister's adroit use of intelligence, in part, to an imaginative and reflective mind.[20]

The correlation between personality type and the capacity to exploit intelligence extends to the operational level of war. Harold Deutsch, in his comparative analysis of intelligence use by World War II generals, concluded that although all commanders were vulnerable to episodes of wishful thinking, the rigid minded were less likely to use intelligence resources effectively.[21] Deutsch identified Field Marshal Erwin Rommel and Gen George Patton as "top practitioners of the creative use of intelligence" who habitually demanded much of their intelligence advisors and were sufficiently flexible to adjust course as intelligence identified potential opportunities and risks.[22]

Despite Patton's gruff public persona, he was collegial with and inquisitive of his intelligence advisors during planning. Maj Melvin Helfers, an intelligence officer who worked for Patton, said of the commander, "My experience with him was like a college professor conducting a seminar, easy going and he had a sense of humor."[23] Additionally, Patton used intelligence to drive his operational planning. As one author noted, "Patton never made a move without first consulting G-2 [his director of intelligence]. G-2 always had the first to say. The usual procedure at other Headquarters was to decide what to do and then, perhaps, ask G-2 what was out front. Patton always got his information first and then acted on the basis of it."[24]

One episode that demonstrates the faith Patton placed in intelligence occurred on the evening of 6 August 1944. Toward the end of the first full week of US Third Army operations in France, Patton ordered advancing forces to stop and reposition defensively around Mortain after receiving notice of a probable German counteroffensive in that area from his director of intelligence, then-colonel Oscar Koch.[25] The Germans attacked the morning of 7

August expecting to find the area unprotected.[26] Instead, they confronted a dug-in 35th Division and a sky filled with combat aircraft.[27] At Mortain the German counteroffensive broke and the door swung open for Patton's drive across France. The conditions for this success were set, in part, by the commander's willingness to adjust plans based on intelligence assessments.

Another example of intelligence-based opportunism by a flexibly minded commander is then-lieutenant general George Kenney's use of airpower in the southwest Pacific. According to Edward Drea, the innovative Kenney capitalized repeatedly on intelligence derived from Japanese military communications—codenamed ULTRA—to orchestrate successful operations.[28] At the Battle of the Bismark Sea in March 1943, intelligence presented Kenney the opportunity to interdict a Japanese convoy carrying the 51st Division to Lae, New Guinea.[29] Drea concluded of the ambush, "Destruction was so complete that the strategic initiative in New Guinea passed forever from Japanese hands."[30] Kenney also demonstrated his willingness to exploit opportunities presented by intelligence in his attacks against Wewak in August 1943, around Rabaul in October and November 1943, and at Hollandia in March and April 1944.[31] Drea noted, "Kenney and his air commanders used ULTRA with deadly effectiveness."[32]

Conversely, some commanders were more rigid in their thinking. Deutsch singled out Field Marshal Bernard Montgomery as an example of an obstinate commander who "brushed aside, with disastrous consequences, [intelligence that] did not suit him in relation to Goodwood, the Antwerp estuary, and Market Garden."[33] Additionally, Drea wrote that the strong-minded Gen Douglas MacArthur's "sense of destiny" shaped his strategic concepts and operational plans more than any intelligence revelations.[34] He disregarded timely and accurate intelligence before undertaking potentially disastrous—although ultimately successful—operations in the Admiralties from February through May 1944, at Leyte in October 1944, at Luzon in January 1945, and in his planning for the invasion of Kyushu in the summer of 1945.[35] According to Drea, "MacArthur consistently dismissed ULTRA evidence that failed to accord with his preconceived strategic vision."[36] Summarizing the role of personality using two archetypes, a determined but unimaginative commander, uncomfortable with uncertainty and impervious to criticism, is less able to exploit intelligence than a supple-minded commander who is alive to change and tolerant of dissenting views.[37]

In addition to personality, the commander's experience also matters. A commander accustomed to employing intelligence at the operational level of war enjoys advantages compared to a counterpart who does not know of the methodologies, possibilities, and limits of operational intelligence. Handel noted that most senior military leaders only experience tactical intelligence before assuming operational-level command, requiring on-the-job-training in the nuances of operational intelligence leadership.[38] While tactical intelligence is immediate and straightforward, operational intelligence requires the commander, in an iterative and time-consuming analytical process, to fully consider longer-term questions, such as what might the enemy do next?[39] Handel contended, "A principal problem senior military commanders face is that experience is normally the only way to acquire a proper education in the use of intelligence on the higher levels of command."[40]

Patton's example supports the contention that experience matters. By the time Patton led the Third Army into Normandy in August 1944, he was a veteran commander of the North Africa and Sicily campaigns and very comfortable with the leadership and consumption of operational intelligence.[41] Furthermore, he had two intelligence assignments earlier in his career that familiarized him with the potential and limitations of intelligence activities.[42]

There is also an attitudinal dimension to a leader's experience with intelligence.[43] Those who attribute previous success to the skillful use of intelligence are far more receptive to advice from intelligence professionals. Contrasting Hitler with Churchill, the former's early experience with German intelligence convinced him that his intuition was more reliable than the prognostications of his military professionals, whereas the latter's extensive familiarity and positive experience with British intelligence products taught him that intelligence actually was vital to the formulation of strategy and the design of campaigns.[44] At the operational level of war, Montgomery's distrust of intelligence advice—which sometimes bordered on hostility—was probably both a cause and an effect of the greater faith he placed in his intuition and exhaustive planning.[45] In contrast, Patton, who often relied on and praised his intelligence staff, said of his intelligence director, "I ought to know what I'm doing; I've got the best damned intelligence officer in any United States command."[46]

Two additional factors—perceptions of vulnerability and expertise—determine the quality of a commander's leadership as it relates to intelligence. First, leaders who perceive their force as being weak compared to an adversary have greater incentive to seek extensive support from intelligence.[47] Handel ascribed this condition to British leadership following the initial setbacks of World War II and to Israeli leadership since 1949.[48]

Similarly, Deutsch noted that offensive-minded commanders lean more heavily on intelligence, perhaps to mitigate the risks of their daring ventures.[49] For example, both Rommel and Patton, who relied on speed and surprise in their operational concepts, were enthusiastic users of intelligence.[50] In North Africa in 1941–42, Rommel supplemented his communications intelligence reports with frequent personal aerial reconnaissance sorties to augment his understanding of the battlespace.[51] He also devised elaborate deception ruses based on his perceptions of the adversary's intelligence collection activities.[52] Patton enhanced his aggressive operations with the systematic use of intelligence. Group Captain Frederick Winterbotham, a senior Royal Air Force officer familiar with ULTRA and Patton, concluded that the American "never failed to use every opportunity that ULTRA gave him to bust open the enemy."[53] Commanders who must optimize resources and action tend to be more open to the opportunities presented by their intelligence than do commanders with force superiorities and passive aims.

In addition, a commander's self-perception of expertise on a matter also affects his or her use of intelligence. In general, leaders who believe themselves already familiar with a situation or issue are less inclined to request advice or consider alternative viewpoints. For this reason, leaders are often more receptive of technical and specialized intelligence, such as scientific or economic assessments.[54] At the operational level of war, commanders are least receptive of battlefield assessments that contradict prevailing opinion. Unfortunately, commanders are not immune to the cognitive pathologies described previously.

The overconfidence that pervaded the 12th Army Group and the First Army before the December 1944 Battle of the Bulge in Belgium's Ardennes forest provides one example of premature cognitive closure. According to John Eisenhower, the steady advance of Allied forces across Western Europe imbued both commanders and intelligence officers with a spirit of optimism that clouded their judgment.[55] Convinced that *Wehrmacht* commanders intended to withdraw to Germany, American leaders dismissed intelligence reports that indicated preparations for a German counteroffensive.[56] A German attack through the Ardennes simply made no sense given the Allied leadership's "predetermination of enemy intentions."[57] Consequently, the assaults that began on 16 December came as a surprise and were a bloody test of Allied mettle that forced American and British commanders to scramble together an operational response. Commanders must be keenly aware of how their personality, experience, and perceptions of expertise affect their judgment, including their use of intelligence. Assisting to this end will be the director of intelligence.

The Intelligence Advisor

The quality of the intelligence advisor also contributes to the success of intelligence at the operational level of war. Directors of intelligence require the ability to gain the commander's trust as well as personal integrity and moral courage, professional expertise, intellectual flexibility, and a talent for communicating. Foremost is gaining trust, without which the advisor lacks access to the decision maker.

Rapport between the commander and intelligence advisor is critical.[58] Advisors require access to the commander to receive guidance and deliver products. Betts argued, "The best analysis is useless if those with authority to act on it do not use it."[59] Leaders can function effectively without positive chemistry with senior intelligence officers; intelligence officers cannot.[60]

Oscar Koch, who served as Patton's long-time director of intelligence and enjoyed an unsurpassed rapport with the commander, called the mutual respect between the commander and intelligence advisor "command support." Koch wrote:

> Command support—the support of his commander, evidenced primarily by mutual confidence engendered by and nurtured through respect. He must be confident that the results of his efforts will be respected by his commander, both in terms of interest and attitude and in the degree of utilization of the end product so painstakingly produced. The commander on the other hand, must be confident that his intelligence chief's work merits such respect. If either confidence fails, command support is nonexistent. With command support, G-2 will tackle any job. Without it, he performs a useless task, merely going through a series of staff exercises. In that case, both he and the commander are losers.[61]

To build the necessary relationship, Handel recommended that senior intelligence officers first endeavor to understand the working habits, character, and ambitions of their commanders.[62] Experience provides intelligence advisors insight into the commander's perspective. Handel concluded, "In the education of the intelligence expert priority should be given to better acquaintance or previous experience with the problems of command and the planning of military operations."[63] Learning to think like the commander enables the advisor to anticipate the principal's challenges and questions, making intelligence more relevant to the decision maker. In this way, familiarity builds trust and credibility.

However, advisors must balance rapport with integrity. Effective intelligence officers guard against excessive familiarity with the commander, which can undermine analytical objectivity.[64] They must also possess the courage to present unfavorable information.[65] Most commanders are not accustomed to receiving criticism of their decisions from subordinates, and honest reporting of the unfavorable consequences of a proposed or actual course of action can constitute an implicit critique.[66]

Furthermore, many commanders commit to a preferred or already chosen course of action. Intelligence assessments support decision making and thus aid the commander by the objective evaluation of plans and policies.[67] Advisors carry a duty to advise honestly, regardless of the popularity of the intelligence at their disposal.[68] For these reasons, strength of character and ethical standards—moral courage—are requisites of effective senior intelligence officers.[69] Successful partnerships between commanders and advisors strike a balance between intimacy and distance and between trust and objectivity.[70]

Expertise, often developed over years of experience, helps advisors build credible partnerships with commanders. Intelligence is a complicated enterprise; senior intelligence officers spend years navigating the archipelago of competing and cooperating intelligence organizations and understanding the processes of collection and analysis. One recent study determined that 90 percent of Air Force intelligence colonels had acquired up to 44 distinct skills during their careers.[71] Expertise postures the advisor to orient intelligence resources to support the commander. It also prepares the senior intelligence officer to educate the commander in how to lead intelligence effectively.[72]

Additionally, the best advisors are analytically flexible. It is axiomatic that they are meticulous and thorough, but they must also possess the capacity to tolerate uncertainty.[73] Intelligence professionals must wage an active and continual battle to mitigate the cognitive pathologies within their minds and organizations. Shlomo Gazit asserted, "Intellectual arrogance is one of the most dangerous qualities for an analyst. Those who are sure of themselves after coming to a decision have no place in intelligence."[74]

Finally, good advisors master the art of communication. They discriminate between the necessary and extraneous, protecting commanders from information overload at the risk of being perceived as withholding intelligence.[75] They compose intelligence products to suit the commander's style, even incorporating showmanship when necessary.[76] Similarly, advisors develop a sense of timing, learning when to present intelligence so that it remains pertinent and within context.[77] In sum, effective advisors distill complex issues into those salient points that are most relevant to the commander and then convey them in a way that assists the commander's understanding of the situation and available options.

Conclusions

Intelligence is not a substitute for the commander's judgment; rather it is an aid to it. Today's operational-level commanders must understand how to exploit intelligence systems as an extension of their minds. The attributes of the commander, the intelligence advisor, and the partnership between them shape the potential for success of intelligence at the operational level of war. The ideal relationship is open, engaging, and mutually respectful without becoming personal. The intelligence advisor belongs within the commander's inner circle yet is permitted a degree of autonomy. The best advisor is analytical, courageous, intellectually flexible, and articulate. The commander, however, is most critical to the success of operational intelligence. Personality, past experience leading intelligence, and self-perceptions of vulnerability and expertise mold the use of intelligence. Open-minded commanders tolerant of uncertainty and alternate viewpoints and familiar with the capabilities and limits of intelligence are best suited to exploit intelligence in their decision making at the operational level of war.

Notes

1. Clausewitz, *On War*, 117.

2. Rosello, "Clausewitz's Contempt," 12; and Goerlitz, *History of the German General Staff*, 61.

3. Rosello, "Clausewitz's Contempt," 12–14; Luvaas, "Napoleon's Use of Intelligence," 40–54; and de Grimoard, "Treatise on Service," 37–40.

4. Brugioni, *Eyes in the Sky*, 1. For example, Exod. 17:8–13 records that Moses watched from a hilltop as Joshua led the Israelites in battle against the Amelekites. Sun Tzu, *Illustrated Art of War*, 236; Caesar, *Caesar's Commentaries*, 7; Austin and Rankov, *Exploratio*, 54–60; Andrew, "American Presidents," 431; Rose, *Washington's Spies*; and Luvaas, "Napoleon's Use of Intelligence," 40–54.

5. Thomas, "U.S. Military Intelligence Analysis," 138; and van Creveld, *Command in War*, 56–57, 66–68.

6. Van Creveld, *Command in War*, 56–57; and Thomas, "U.S. Military Intelligence Analysis," 138.

7. Showalter, "Intelligence on the Eve," 25; Kahn, *Codebreakers*, ix, 119; and Kennett, *First Air War*, 23.

8. Owens, "Emerging System of Systems," 15; Libicki, *Mesh and the Net*, 24; Libicki, "DBK and its Consequences," 28; and Handel, *Intelligence and Military Operations*, 12.

9. The author perceives an unsurprising scholarship imbalance that tilts toward decisions and processes at the strategic level of war. He attributes the relative breadth and depth of the strategic literature over that on the operational level of war to four factors. (1) The operational level is a recent advent in Anglo-American doctrine. Therefore, its direct assessment is relatively new. While previous historical works implicitly consider it, they seldom separate the operational level from the strategic or tactical. (2) The relative profile of strategic-level issues and personalities garners more attention, therefore more scholarship. (3) While the classified nature of intelligence limits research on its role in decision making across all levels of war, the higher profile of strategic-level issues places greater pressure on government offices to declassify materials related to momentous decisions. (4) Strategic-level decisions tend to produce more evidence than those at the operational level of war. The pace, conditions, and diffractive nature of information during war make operational-level record keeping relatively less comprehensive. As well, to the extent strategic-level decision making is more plural, it has the potential to produce a greater number of accounts on key decisions. That is not to say that worthy

works do not exist on decisions and personalities at the operational level of war; rather, only that the strategic literature may supplement our understanding of the latter.

10. Handel, *Leaders and Intelligence*, 6.

11. Gazit, "Intelligence Estimates," 267.

12. Handel, *Leaders and Intelligence*, 6.

13. Blakesley, *Presidential Leadership*, 7.

14. George and George, *Presidential Personality*, 9. For more information, see Barber, *Presidential Character*; Neustadt, *Presidential Power*; and Buchanan, *Citizen's Presidency*.

15. George and George, *Presidential Personality*, 9.

16. Ibid.

17. Jablonsky, "Paradox of Duality," 55–117.

18. Ibid., 75.

19. Ibid.

20. Andrew, "Churchill and Intelligence" 181–93.

21. Deutsch, "Commanding Generals," 254–55.

22. Ibid., 255.

23. Shwedo, *XIX Tactical Air Command*, 24.

24. Allen, *Lucky Forward*, 68.

25. Deutsch, "Commanding Generals," 230; and Shwedo, *XIX Tactical Air Command*, 46–51.

26. Deutsch, "Commanding Generals," 230; and Shwedo, *XIX Tactical Air Command*, 50.

27. Shwedo, *XIX Tactical Air Command*, 50.

28. Drea, *MacArthur's ULTRA*, 232. For a useful biography of Kenney, which extols his flexible mind and innovative character, see Thomas E. Griffith, Jr., *MacArthur's Airman: General George C. Kenney and the War in the Southwest Pacific* (Lawrence, KS: University of Kansas Press, 1998).

29. Ibid., 61, 68–71.

30. Ibid., 61.

31. Ibid., 232. According to Drea, Kenney had his own cognitive blinders. One documented case of Kenney's disregard for intelligence occurred in his assessment of Japanese defenses in the Admiralties. Following a series of bombing attacks on the islands, Kenney concluded that the islands were deserted and strongly recommended their invasion to MacArthur. Kenney based his analysis on reports from a limited number of aerial reconnaissance flights that revealed no activity. As well, his conviction in the efficacy of air power may have skewed his thinking. Kenney's assessment contradicted that of MacArthur's director of intelligence, then-colonel Charles Willoughby. Based on multiple sources, the intelligence estimate concluded that a substantial Japanese force remained to defend the Admiralties. Kenney refused to believe Willoughby's assessments, which turned out to be remarkably accurate. Despite this example of wishful thinking by Kenney, Drea concluded that, in sum, the Airman was willing to exploit the opportunities offered by intelligence. For a description of Kenney's faulty analysis, see Drea, *MacArthur's ULTRA*, 98–104.

32. Ibid., 232.

33. Deutsch, "Commanding Generals," 254.

34. Drea, *MacArthur's ULTRA*, 230.

35. Ibid., 231.

36. Ibid., 230.

37. Handel, *Leaders and Intelligence*, 6.

38. Ibid., 16.

39. Ibid., 27.

40. Ibid., 25.

41. Deutsch, "Commanding Generals," 230.

42. Nye, *Patton Mind*, 67, 102; Koch and Hays, *G-2*, 150–64; and Shwedo, *XIX Tactical Air Command*, 17, 132.

43. Handel, *Leaders and Intelligence*, 7.

44. Ibid.; and Andrew, "Churchill and Intelligence," 181–85.

45. Deutsch, "Commanding Generals," 211–15.

46. Ayer, *Before the Colors Fade*, 175; and Shwedo, *XIX Tactical Air Command*, 17–18.

47. Handel, *Leaders and Intelligence*, 7.

48. Ibid., 7–8.

49. Ibid., 29–30; and Deutsch, "Commanding Generals," 255.

50. Deutsch, "Commanding Generals," 229.

51. Ibid., 215–16.

52. Ibid., 216.

53. Winterbotham, *ULTRA Secret*, 151; Deutsch, "Commanding Generals," 229; and Shwedo, *XIX Tactical Air Command*, 13.

54. Handel, *Leaders and Intelligence*, 8.

55. Eisenhower, *Bitter Woods*, 168.

56. Ibid., 162–78. Particularly noteworthy are the assessments of Col Monk Dickson, including Estimate 37 dated 10 December 1944. Although not entirely accurate, Dickson forecasted the German counteroffensive.

57. Ibid., 168, 174.

58. Gazit, "Intelligence Estimates," 268.

59. Betts, *Enemies of Intelligence*, 67; and Betts, "New Politics of Intelligence," 7.

60. Handel, *Leaders and Intelligence*, 15; and Gazit, "Intelligence Estimates," 268.

61. Koch and Hays, *G-2*, 165; and Shwedo, *XIX Tactical Air Command*, 127.

62. Handel, *Intelligence and Military Operations*, 28.

63. Ibid., 31.

64. Kent, *Strategic Intelligence*, 195–206. Kent argued that intelligence organizations required a measure of autonomy from decision makers to safeguard analytical integrity. Politicization and pandering are two potential pitfalls of insufficient autonomy. The former occurs when strategic intelligence advisors become invested in (or are perceived to be invested in) a policy option or policy maker. Commanders and courses of action can similarly co-opt operational intelligence advisors. For more on politicization see Gates, "Guarding against Politicization," 5–13; Ransom, "Politicization of Intelligence," 171–82; Betts, *Enemies of Intelligence*, 66–103; and Treverton, "Intelligence Analysis," 91–104. Pandering means intelligence is shaped to curry favor with a decision maker. For more on pandering, see Wirtz, "Intelligence to Please?," 183–97; and Westerfield, "Inside Ivory Bunkers," 198–218.

65. Jones, "Intelligence and Command," 291.

66. Handel, *Intelligence and Military Operations*, 28.

67. Handel, "*Leaders and Intelligence*," 9.

68. Ibid.

69. Handel, *Intelligence and Military Operations*, 31.

70. Gazit, "Intelligence Estimates," 263–69. He called the partnership a "reciprocal relationship."

71. Brauner, Massey, Moore, and Medlin, *Improving Development and Utilization*, 24.

72. Handel, *Leaders and Intelligence*, 15; and Gazit, "Intelligence Estimates," 273.

73. Gazit, "Estimates and Fortune-Telling," 39.

74. Ibid.

75. Handel, *Leaders and Intelligence*, 31; and Jones, "Intelligence and Command," 292–93.

76. Handel, *Intelligence and Military Operations*, 28–32; and Jones, "Intelligence and Command," 292–94.

77. Jones, "Intelligence and Command," 294–95.

Chapter 5

Operational Intelligence in the Malayan Emergency

The Emergency will be won by our intelligence system.

—Sir Gerald Templer

The Malayan Emergency is an intelligence success story.[1] After assuming the combined positions of United Kingdom high commissioner and director of operations for Malaya in 1952, Gen Sir Gerald Templer predicted that the emergency would be won by intelligence.[2] Anthony Short, in his authoritative history of the emergency, agreed with Templer when he concluded, "the key to counter insurgency in Malaya was intelligence."[3] Precisely how significant it was, relative to other factors, remains a disputed point. Others highlight the pivotal role of hearts and minds, population control, leadership, organizational culture, and the overarching policies of decolonization and Malayanization.[4] Nonetheless, intelligence was a crucial factor in the eventual success of the British-led counterinsurgency.

This chapter evaluates the evolution and contributions of intelligence during the 1948–60 Malayan Emergency. It begins with a brief overview of the emergency, which identifies three broad periods, key decisions, and principal leaders. Next, it describes the evolution of collection and analysis during these periods and highlights intelligence shortcomings and successes. The chapter concludes that the emergency's turning point resulted from the dynamic execution of a good plan that was informed by improving intelligence and led by commanders who fully appreciated the advantages and limits of intelligence at the operational level of war.

An Overview of the Emergency

The Malayan Emergency can be divided into three broad phases.[5] It began in June 1948 when Sir Edward Gent, the UK high commissioner of Malaya, declared a state of emergency following the murders of three European planters and their Chinese assistants.[6] At the time, the incident was the most recent in a rising tide of post–World War II violence perpetrated by the Malayan Communist Party (MCP)–led insurgency.[7] During this early phase, the British employed a counterterrorism strategy designed to intimidate the Chinese population of Malaya into submission.[8] It proved ineffective.

The arrival of Lt Gen Sir Harold Briggs as director of operations on 3 April 1950 marked the start of the emergency's second phase. He conceptualized the challenge as a competition in government.[9] With High Commissioner Sir Henry Gurney's endorsement, Briggs unveiled a scheme—subsequently known as the Briggs Plan—to isolate the MCP.[10] The plan is best known for its controversial resettlement of 500,000 Chinese squatters into "New Villages."[11] However, its central aim was to extend governmental control by enfranchising the Chinese population through improved governance and strengthened local administration.[12] Briggs also introduced a committee system at the federal, state, and district levels to improve governmental coordination and decision making.[13] When Briggs retired in December 1951, he left behind the plan and basic organizational structure for success.[14] Despite these positive steps, Malaya's future appeared uncertain.[15]

In February 1952 Templer replaced Briggs and Gurney.[16] He endorsed the Briggs Plan as his operational prescription and helped energize the struggle against the insurgents with obvious dynamism.[17] He oversaw the completion of resettlement and initiated further reorganization of key governmental functions, including intelligence. Templer's dynamic implementation of the Briggs Plan broke the insurgency before he departed Malaya in 1954.[18]

The emergency's tipping point, brought about by the leadership of both Briggs and Templer, occurred between 1951 and 1952, in the middle of the second phase.[19] Most security indicators began dramatic, steady improvement during Templer's first year in office. For example, the number of annual incidents and casualties both hit highwater marks in 1951 before falling by almost half in 1952.[20] Insurgent strength also peaked in 1951.[21] Such statistical indicators, coupled with the assassination of Gurney in October 1951, obscured signs of progress before Briggs's departure.[22] British and Malay leadership were very concerned with the state of affairs as they searched for Briggs's replacement.[23]

In retrospect, tentative counterinsurgency gains were evident in early to mid 1951.[24] The MCP strategy offers some evidence of this reality. Chinese resettlement, designed to constrain popular and logistical support to the MCP, began in June 1950 and was almost complete when Briggs left Malaya.[25] The MCP responded to the Briggs Plan with an August 1950 "Guide to the Anti-Resettlement Campaign," which ordered maximum resistance and precipitated the record violence of 1951.[26] However, by late 1951 MCP leaders worried that indiscriminate violence alienated the civilians upon whom the party depended.[27] Its "October [1951] Resolutions" reemphasized political mobilization and directed more selective attacks against "imperialist" targets that would not harm the masses.[28] Chen Peng, the MCP's secretary-general, later claimed that the insurgency was most hopeful in 1949–50, before resettlement began to constrict its support.[29] Thus, the MCP's strategic adjustments in late 1951 partly explain the reduced levels of violence in 1952 and suggest that the emergency may have been approaching its climax during Briggs's tenure.

Other indicators corroborate 1951 as the beginning of the counterinsurgency's seizure of initiative. According to a 1952 intelligence assessment, MCP casualty rates steadily increased from April 1950 to September 1951.[30] Additionally, the number of contacts per month between government and insurgent forces rose from approximately 60 in July 1950 to 150 in January 1951, remained steady through 1952, and then began a permanent decline by early 1953. Additionally, the insurgent-government kill ratio, which was at its lowest in 1950, began improving in 1951.[31] Clearly, under the leadership of both Briggs and Templer, counterinsurgency forces became increasingly efficient in their work.

During the emergency's final phase, which followed Templer's tenure, there was continued progress in Malayan governance and security.[32] The characterization of this period as a "mopping-up effort" undervalues the challenges of a political consolidation that secured an enduring peace.[33] The government's steady exploitation of its gains prevented recalcitrant remnants of the MCP from revitalizing the insurgency and ensured that the Malayan Emergency situation gradually returned to normal.

The Evolution of Intelligence during the Emergency

Counterinsurgency progress in Malaya corresponded with dramatic improvements in intelligence. The intelligence system was portrayed as deficient in 1948 and optimal by the emergency's latter stages.[34] Three moments—the beginnings of the emergency's three phases—best illustrate this evolution.

At the emergency's outset, the British intelligence system condition in Malaya was woeful.[35] It was underorganized, underresourced, and ineffectively led. The fragmented intelligence community consisted of the Malayan Security Service (MSS), that generated assessments; the police's new Special Branch (SB), created in August 1948, that informed criminal investigations; and intelligence elements within military units, that advised commanders on matters of tactical employment. Little, if any, coordination existed among them.[36]

Furthermore, the organizations were small and had only limited capacity.[37] For example, the SB consisted of 12 officers and 44 inspectors.[38] Very few government officials knew Chinese.[39] Finally, and perhaps most important, the pre-1948 British intelligence system in Malaya did not focus on the MCP or insurgency, concentrating instead on pan-Malay nationalism, which was perceived as the most significant threat to the Crown's imperial position.[40] Riley Sunderland, who wrote a 1964 analysis of intelligence in Malaya, summarized the situation: "In 1948 . . . intelligence on the communist terrorists and their sympathizers was haphazard, uncoordinated, and poorly used."[41]

Consequently, the intelligence system could not support either operational or tactical requirements.[42] Assessments of the insurgent situation were glaringly inaccurate. One MSS estimate, dated two days before Gent declared the state of emergency, concluded, "the immediate threat to internal security is negligible."[43] Initial reports underestimated the threat and persistently mischaracterized the communist insurgents as bandits.[44]

Intelligence in the field was as inadequate as at the headquarters.[45] The system could not generate the information needed for effective military operations.[46] Large-scale sweeps of the jungle by infantry battalions seldom produced contact with guerrilla forces.[47] One infantry battalion commander lamented, "There is no intelligence worth the name."[48] Thus, the British began implementing their initial counterterrorism strategy without an adequate understanding of the environment, the adversary, or the problem.[49]

British authorities had recognized the systemic intelligence shortfall in Malaya for years.[50] A 1946 report by the inspector general of police urged the creation of a pan-Malayan intelligence organization.[51] Even the British Cabinet commented on the need to develop better intelligence in Malaya.[52] Nevertheless, the system received little emphasis beyond an initial 1948 reorganization.[53] Additionally, the blunt counterterrorism strategy increasingly alienated the Chinese population, limiting their cooperation with governmental authorities and denying a crucial potential intelligence source.

British intelligence in Malaya was still declining in 1950 when Briggs conceptualized his successful plan at the start of the emergency's second phase.[54] Upon arriving in April, he conducted an extensive tour of the federation to form his own appreciation of the challenge.[55] It is arguable that, with two years of accrued experience, intelligence analysts and their assessments also contributed to Briggs's balanced understanding of the MCP and battlespace.[56] Nevertheless, he was sufficiently unimpressed by the intelligence system, labeling it the emergency's Achilles heel, and immediately corrected it.[57]

Briggs instituted several structural improvements to intelligence during his tenure. By May 1950 he established a federal intelligence advisory committee to facilitate the sharing of critical information among government agencies.[58] In August he created the director of intelligence position to coordinate all collection and analytical activities and appointed the head of the SB, Sir William Jenkin, to this dual role.[59] Briggs also presided over the expansion of the SB and the creation of its training school.[60] Furthermore, on the tactical front, he issued guidance for military units to replace large-unit sweeps with smaller, intelligence-led operations.[61] The cumulative effects of intelligence take time, and the benefits of Briggs's organizational changes were not immediate.[62] Nevertheless, by late 1951 the increasing efficiency of counterinsurgency efforts suggests an enhanced understanding of the situation by British authorities.

Like Briggs, Templer understood the importance of intelligence.[63] Granted sweeping powers as high commissioner and director of operations, he consolidated and expanded the organizational changes of his predecessor.[64] He also made intelligence, including penetration of the MCP, the principal aim of all counterinsurgency activity.[65] Templer made intelligence his "absolute top priority."[66]

Templer's faith stemmed from his familiarity with intelligence. In addition to exploiting and consuming intelligence as a commander at various levels within the British armed forces, he also served multiple assignments within the intelligence community. Templer led the collection and analysis of intelligence in support of operations as deputy director of intelligence at the General Headquarters of the British Expeditionary Force in Western Europe from 1938 until 1940.[67] The German army's rapid advance through the Low Countries and the British evacuation from Dunkirk probably left an indelible impression with him on both the advantages and limits of intelligence. In 1946 Templer returned to the War Office as the director of military intelligence.[68] Furthermore, as vice chief of the Imperial General Staff between 1948 and 1950, Templer kept British military intelligence as part of his portfolio.[69] By his appointment to Malaya in 1952, Templer was very familiar with all aspects of intelligence activity and well postured to optimize the system in Malaya. "As a former DMI [director of military intelligence]," Templer asserted, "I know my onions."[70]

Templer consolidated and expanded the organizational changes of his predecessor. Before he appointed Jack Morton as director of intelligence on 1 April 1952, Templer made the position a standing member of the director of operations committee and placed it on par with the service and bureaucracy chiefs.[71] He also required that the services submit all operations plans to the director of intelligence for review.[72] Templer separated the positions of director of intelligence and chief of the SB, empowering the former to coordinate and evaluate all intelligence activities in Malaya.[73] The division of labor freed the director of intelligence to concentrate on operational-level analysis and support to the commander and staff; it also permitted the SB to focus on collection operations against the MCP.[74] Later in 1952, the position of the SB was elevated within police headquarters to provide a broadened aperture and facilitate support relationships.[75] Finally, during Templer's tenure, the army augmented the SB with intelligence officers to facilitate reporting from and planning support to tactical forces.[76] Together with his intelligence director, Templer galvanized the Malayan intelligence system into an effective information gathering and analysis organization.

From his years of experience, Templer understood the critical, special relationship between a commander and the director of intelligence. He invigorated the position in several ways, but perhaps most importantly, he maintained an open and direct channel between himself and his principal intelligence advisor.[77] Templer chose his advisor carefully. Morton was a civilian and a career intelligence officer with years of experience in the region who had most recently led the Singapore branch of the British security service known as MI5.[78] He was the chief architect of many of Templer's organizational changes.[79] He also became part of Templer's inner circle and one of his most intimate advisors.[80] "Mind you," Templer told Morton, "we've got to like each other. It won't work otherwise."[81] By the time of his departure in 1954, Templer had instilled confidence and dynamism into the intelligence system, as he did throughout Malaya.

Morton informed the commander about the operational planning process; the SB worked to improve what was known about the MCP and overall situation. Only the SB had the authority to operate secret agents.[82] It also became the central clearinghouse for all captured and surrendered MCP documents and personnel.[83] As the SB built a clear understanding of the insurgency, its efforts focused on penetrating guerilla cells with spies. Furthermore, its analytical products became the well from which Morton's advice drew. The SB also provided army units increasingly detailed assessments with which to plan tactical operations.[84]

Tactical commanders in Malaya combined the intelligence received from the SB with the background information they assembled while patrolling their assigned districts.[85] They performed their own analysis to deduce the likely locations and times of MCP activity and supplemented this with information from local sources among the population. Furthermore, when ambushes and other discreet operations failed to make contact with the enemy, they narrowed the search. Contact, or the lack of it, helped to build an increased understanding of MCP activity in the area.[86] In this way intelligence from operational-level organizations enabled tactical action.[87]

During the emergency's third phase, the intelligence system generated a steady stream of accurate, actionable intelligence. Gone were the generalities characteristic of early intelligence reports. Instead, assessments detailed MCP organizational structure, locations, and, most impressively, the identities of known and suspected guerrillas.[88] One staff review in the late 1950s credited intelligence with initiating the vast majority of contacts between security forces and the MCP, resulting in the capture or killing of guerrillas.[89] Comfortable with their understanding of the conflict and the increasing gains in security, British authorities shifted their focus to the Malayanization of governance and the decolonization of Malaya that preserved the peace.

Conclusions

The Malayan Emergency is an intelligence success story. However, the positive correlation between the effectiveness of the overall counterinsurgency effort and the effectiveness of the intelligence system during the Malayan Emergency does not suggest a straightforward causal relationship. Intelligence, operations, and several other factors interacted in multifarious and mutually reinforcing ways. Psychological operations to win hearts and minds, population control through resettlement and food rationing, the dynamic leadership of Templer, British organizational learning, and the policies of decolonization and Malayanization also contributed to the emergency's successful conclusion. Nevertheless, the correlation between intelligence and counterinsurgency is impressive. As intelligence improved, security did as well. As security improved, Chinese civilians provided the information needed to defeat the insurgency. Thus, there was a naturally reinforcing relationship between operational effectiveness and intelligence effectiveness.

At the emergency's outbreak, intelligence and security operations were in disarray. During the late 1940s, British intelligence failed to recognize the emergence of a communist insurgency. Additionally, its insufficient understanding of the problem contributed to a counterterrorism strategy that delayed progress by about two years. The intelligence system in Malaya was still in poor condition when Briggs arrived in 1950. It remains unclear whether his prescient conceptualization of the environment and problem was informed by improving assessments or he conducted the analysis himself. It is clear that Briggs placed enormous importance on intelligence and improved the system to the extent he could given his limited authority. Among his most important reforms was the creation of the director-of-intelligence position to shoulder the responsibilities that lay beyond tactical-level intelligence. Despite the limitations to Briggs's authority, he conceived and began to implement the plan that would set the conditions for success. Templer's energetic execution of the Briggs Plan produced substantial counterinsurgency gains. Furthermore, his progressive intelligence reforms invigorated and functionalized both intelligence and operations. He enhanced the former by removing bureaucratic obstacles to effective collection and analysis. Meanwhile, he improved operations by making intelligence integral to planning and execution. Templer's experience with and appreciation of intelligence prepared him to effectively lead his intelligence apparatus. He did so in collaboration with an empowered and capable director of intelligence, with whom he enjoyed the special relationship critical to the success of intelligence at the operational level of war.

Notes

1. Stewart, "Winning in Malaya," 268.
2. Cloake, *Templer*, 227.
3. Short, *Communist Insurrection in Malaya*; and Stewart, "Winning in Malaya," 268.
4. For the role of the hearts and minds effort, see Stubbs, *Hearts and Minds*. For population control, see Hack, "Malayan Emergency," 383–414. For leadership, see Smith, "General Templer and Counter-Insurgency," 60–78. For organizational culture, see Nagl, *Learning to Eat Soup*. For British policies, see Stockwell, "British Imperial Policy," 68–87; and Stockwell, "Insurgency and Decolonisation," 71–81.
5. Thompson, *Defeating Communist Insurgency*, 16; and Clutterbuck, *Long Long War*, 4–5. Thompson and Clutterbuck divided the insurgency into periods of defense (1948–51), offense (1952–54), and victory (1955–60). Their second phase coincided with Templer's tenure, whose contributions they concluded were instrumental to the counterinsurgency's success. R. W. Komer offered a periodization that roughly reflected military leadership changes: 1948–49, 1950–52, 1952–54, and 1954–60. See Komer, *Malayan Emergency in Retrospect*. Karl Hack's phasing aligns with British strategies: 1948–49 (counterterrorism), 1950–52 (clear and hold), and 1952–60 (optimization). See Hack, "Malayan Emergency," 383–414. Like Hack, this author also distinguishes emergency periods as a function of British strategy but prefers to expand the crucial second phase to include the tenures of both Briggs and Templer: 1948–50 (counterterrorism), 1950–54 (population control), and 1954–60 (consolidation).
6. CO 717/167/52849/2/1948, f302, [Declaration of Emergency] Inward Telegram no. 641 from Sir E. Gent to Mr Creech Jones, 17 June 1948, in Stockwell, *British Documents*, 19–20; and Coates, *Suppressing Insurgency*, 7–8.
7. Komer, *Malayan Emergency in Retrospect*, 4.
8. Bennett, " 'A Very Salutary Effect,' " 417.
9. Short, "Communism and the Emergency," 155; Clutterbuck, *Long Long War*, 57; and Coates, *Suppressing Insurgency*, 82.
10. Most of the literature credits Briggs with the plan to isolate the insurgency by resettling Chinese squatters and improving governance. An exception is Noel Barber, who attributes to Gurney the ideas that the emergency was a struggle for political control and that resettlement would simultaneously integrate Malayan society and disrupt MCP support. Barber also attributes the plan's authorship to Sir Robert Thompson. Barber, *War of the Running Dogs*, 61–71, 93–100.
11. Clutterbuck, *Long Long War*, 57.

12. CAB 21/1681, MAL C(50)23, Appendix, "Federation Plan for the Elimination of the Communist Organization and Armed Forces in Malaya" (the Briggs Plan): Report by COS for Cabinet Malaya Committee, 24 May 1950, in Stockwell, *British Documents*, 216–21; and Coates, *Suppressing Insurgency*, 81–84.

13. Coates, *Suppressing Insurgency*, 85.

14. Ibid., 9; Purcell, *Malaya*, 5–19; and Hack, "British Intelligence and Counter-Insurgency," 145.

15. Coates, *Suppressing Insurgency*, 109–11; and Smith, "General Templer and Counter-Insurgency," 63–64.

16. Ramakrishna, "'Transmogrifying' Malaya," 82.

17. Ibid., 83; and Coates, *Suppressing Insurgency*, 118.

18. Thompson, *Defeating Communist Insurgency*, 45; Stubbs, *Hearts and Minds*, 194; Coates, *Suppressing Insurgency*, 4; and Smith, "General Templer and Counter-Insurgency," 61.

19. *Tipping point* refers to the concept that a buildup of small forces within a system can gradually reach a point at which the system tips irreversibly toward a certain outcome. See Gladwell, *Tipping Point*.

20. Hack, "Malayan Emergency," 390–91.

21. Coates, *Suppressing Insurgency*, 69, 76.

22. Ibid., 109. Gurney became a target of opportunity on 6 October 1951 when his motorcade stumbled into an ambush intended to capture a police ammunition convoy. Although a fortunate accident for MCP forces, the event reinforced British perceptions of deteriorating control in Malaya.

23. CAB 129/48, C(51)26, "The Situation in Malaya": Cabinet Memorandum by Mr. Lyttelton, Annexes I-III, 20 Nov 1951, in Stockwell, *British Documents*, 310–15.

24. Stubbs, *Hearts and Minds*, 159; and Hack, "Malayan Emergency," 402.

25. Komer, *Malayan Emergency in Retrospect*, 55.

26. Hack, "Malayan Emergency," 389.

27. Ibid., 390; Short, "Communism and the Emergency," 158; and Barber, *War of the Running Dogs*, 134.

28. Barber, *War of the Running Dogs*, 134; and Hack, "Malayan Emergency," 390.

29. Hack, "Malayan Emergency," 397.

30. Ibid., 401.

31. Ibid., 403.

32. Clutterbuck, *Long Long War*, 5.

33. Several authors, especially those who attribute the counterinsurgency's success to Templer, describe the emergency's later years dismissively. For example, see Thompson, *Defeating Communist Insurgency*, 16; and Komer, *Malayan Emergency in Retrospect*, 21. Conversely, Kumar Ramakrishna avers that the finalization of a political settlement and reconciliation between warring factions were not a foregone conclusion. See Ramakrishna, "Content, Credibility and Context," 242–66.

34. Sunderland, "Antiguerrilla Intelligence in Malaya," v; Bennett, "'A Very Salutary Effect,'" 421; and Hack, "British Intelligence and Counter-Insurgency," 127.

35. Bennett, "'A Very Salutary Effect,'" 420.

36. Hack, "British Intelligence and Counter-Insurgency," 128, 132.

37. Stewart, "Winning in Malaya," 268.

38. Hack, "British Intelligence and Counter-Insurgency," 128.

39. Sunderland, "Antiguerrilla Intelligence in Malaya," 4; Stewart, "Winning in Malaya," 270; and Bennett, "'A Very Salutary Effect,'" 422.

40. Coates, *Suppressing Insurgency*, 25–28.

41. Sunderland, "Antiguerrilla Intelligence in Malaya," v, 6.

42. Bennett, "'A Very Salutary Effect,'" 418.

43. Coates, *Suppressing Insurgency*, 25; and Stewart, "Winning in Malaya," 268.

44. Sunderland, "Antiguerrilla Intelligence in Malaya," 6.

45. Ibid., 9.

46. Bennett, "'A Very Salutary Effect,'" 418.

47. Clutterbuck, *Long Long War*, 42–54; Komer, *Malayan Emergency in Retrospect*, 18; and Hack, "Corpses, Prisoners of War," 215.

48. Sunderland, "Antiguerrilla Intelligence in Malaya," 10.

49. Coates, *Suppressing Insurgency*, 79; and Bennett, "'A Very Salutary Effect,'" 417–18.

50. Stewart, "Winning in Malaya," 268.

51. Coates, *Suppressing Insurgency*, 24.

52. Stockwell, *British Documents*, lxiv.

53. Coates, *Suppressing Insurgency*, 25; and Hack, "British Intelligence and Counter-Insurgency," 127.

54. Hack, "Corpses, Prisoners of War," 214–15.

55. Coates, *Suppressing Insurgency*, 81–82.

56. While British intelligence in Malaya was imperfect when Briggs arrived in 1950, circumstantial evidence suggests it was improving. Two related points support this conclusion. First, the primary source of intelligence on the MCP during the early years of the Malayan Emergency came from the interrogations and documents of captured and surrendered enemy personnel (CEP/SEP). According to British records, from 1948 through March 1950—the month before Briggs arrived in Malaya—there were 1,293 CEP/SEP (783 captured; 510 surrendered) in custody. Second, a review of British assessments of the emergency between 1948 and 1950 suggests an increasingly refined appreciation of the situation. As an example, John Strachey, the British secretary of state for war, circulated an insightful assessment of the emergency that resulted from the analysis of a captured MCP pamphlet entitled "Present Day Situation and Duties." According to A. J. Stockwell, the pamphlet was written in June 1949, captured later that year, transmitted to London in November, and reached the secretary's attention in May 1950. The Briggs Plan and its prescient assessment was also written in May 1950. For an insightful analysis on the MCP and the emergency derived from interviews with SEPs, see Pye, *Guerrilla Communism in Malaya*, 115–342. For more on the importance of SEPs to the practice of intelligence, see Clutterbuck, *Long Long War*, 101–11; Barber, *War of the Running Dogs*, 112–16; Komer, *Malayan Emergency in Retrospect*, 72–75; and Hack, "Corpses, Prisoners of War." For British statistics on captured and enemy personnel, see Coates, *Suppressing Insurgency*, 190–202. For a copy of Mr. Strachey's assessment, see PREM 8/1406/2, MAL C(50)12, "The Present Day Situation and Duties of the Malayan Communist Party": note by Mr Strachey for the Cabinet Malaya Committee Commenting on a Captured MCP document, 12 May 1950, in Stockwell, *British Documents*, 213–16.

57. Hack, "British Intelligence and Counter-Insurgency," 128.

58. Ibid.; and Nagl, *Learning to Eat Soup*, 71.

59. Hack, "British Intelligence and Counter-Insurgency," 129.

60. Ibid., 128–29; and Cloake, *Templer*, 231.

61. Komer, *Malayan Emergency in Retrospect*, 50–51.

OPERATIONAL INTELLIGENCE IN THE MALAYAN EMERGENCY

62. Short, *Communist Insurrection in Malaya*, 359; and Nagl, *Learning to Eat Soup*, 92.

63. Sunderland, "Antiguerrilla Intelligence in Malaya," vi–vii.

64. Ibid., 19.

65. Ibid., vii.

66. Cloake, *Templer*, 227.

67. Ibid., 66–92; and Coates, *Suppressing Insurgency*, 112.

68. Cloake, *Templer*, 168–73; Coates, *Suppressing Insurgency*, 113.

69. Cloake, *Templer*, 173–87.

70. Ibid., 228.

71. CO 1022/60, no 3, [Reorganisation of Government]: Inward Telegram no 268 from Sir G Templer to Mr Lyttelton On New Measures, 28 Feb 1952, in Stockwell, *British Documents*, 373–76; Short, *Communist Insurrection in Malaya*, 360; Cloake, *Templer*, 229; Coates, *Suppressing Insurgency*, 124; and Nagl, *Learning to Eat Soup*, 92.

72. Cloake, *Templer*, 229.

73. Sunderland, "Antiguerrilla Intelligence in Malaya," 26; and Cloake, *Templer*, 229.

74. Sunderland, "Antiguerrilla Intelligence in Malaya," 19–21.

75. Ibid., 23; and Stewart, "Winning in Malaya," 279.

76. Sunderland, "Antiguerrilla Intelligence in Malaya," 27.

77. Cloake, *Templer*, 228.

78. MI5 is military intelligence, Section 5, which performs British counterintelligence activities. See Cloake, *Templer*, 228–30; Coates, *Suppressing Insurgency*, 124; and Nagl, *Learning to Eat Soup*, 91.

79. Cloake, *Templer*, 228–29.

80. Ibid., 229.

81. Ibid.

82. Sunderland, "Antiguerrilla Intelligence in Malaya," 21.

83. Ibid.

84. Kitson, *Low Intensity Operations*, 96.

85. Ibid., 96–97.

86. Ibid., 97–98.

87. For examples of how intelligence enabled tactical action, see the scenario provided in Kitson, *Low Intensity Operations*, 102–31; and the anecdotes recorded in Clutterbuck, *Long Long War*, 101–31.

88. Sunderland, "Antiguerrilla Intelligence in Malaya," 56–63.

89. Ibid., 1.

Chapter 6

Design

If I always appear prepared, it is because before entering an undertaking, I have meditated long and have foreseen what might occur. It is not genius [that] reveals to me suddenly and secretly what I should do in circumstances unexpected by others; it is thought and preparation.

—Napoleon Bonaparte

If you ask the wrong question, you are certain to come up with the wrong answer.

—Colin S. Gray
Stability Operations in Strategic Perspective

Napoleon Bonaparte's coup d'oeil was the subject of legend. His disciple Baron Antoine-Henri de Jomini described it as the ability to form reasonable suppositions about the future despite the uncertainties of the present, and he concluded that this learnable skill was "the most valuable characteristic of a good general."[1] Probably with Napoleon in mind Carl von Clausewitz asserted that genius was "the harmonious combination" of intellect and determination that "rises above all rules."[2] As for the Corsican, Bonaparte attributed his talent of foresight to his capacity for reflection.[3]

The future success of the American armed forces will depend largely on the capacity of its commanders and organizations to reflect. The psychologist David Campbell, in his decades-long study of US Army general officers, identified a common personality profile, which he labeled "aggressive adventurer."[4] These outstanding Americans were dominant, competitive, action-oriented, patriotic, and drawn to physically adventurous activities.[5] Reflection was not a prevalent characteristic.[6] As Lt Gen Walter F. Ulmer Jr. argued in a 1998 article on military leadership, the traits of the aggressive adventurer are ideal for "heroic competence on the battlefield" but misplaced in situations that require "contemplation before action, patience with ambiguity, and an appreciation for broad participation in the decision-making process."[7] The arena Ulmer described was that of modern strategy formulation. If military leaders are not predisposed to be reflective strategists, can structured cognitive processes help compensate?

Charting a course through an uncertain future is not peculiar to military professionals. Leaders in government, business, and academe must also navigate their organizations through difficult challenges and complex situations. Most leaders intuitively grasp that choosing a direction without first knowing what lies ahead can lead to disastrous consequences. To compensate, leaders can bolster their powers of anticipation by employing analysts. However, like their leaders, professional analysts are only as good as the questions they ask.[8] With an endless assortment of potential problems and possible futures, how can strategic thinkers have a decent assurance that they are asking the right questions?

One answer is design, which is the topic of this chapter. The chapter begins by explaining uncertainty and complexity through the lens of systems theory, which is the theoretical underpinning of design. Next, it considers the complexity of social systems and their perversely ill-structured or so-called "wicked" problems. It describes design as a highly complex mental process that imagines the future, reflects on the past, and produces an understanding of both the problem and the optimal solution. The chapter concludes that design is a problem-solving method equipped to help manage the uncertainty and complexity of our world and useful in identifying and addressing complex problems.

Uncertainty, Complexity, and Systems Theory

Because the design discourse draws upon and exists alongside systems, information, complexity, and social theories, it will be useful to introduce a few key concepts. Much is written on these subjects that requires no repetition.[9] Even a synopsis is beyond this work's scope. Thus, the following outlines only a few basic touch points for later evaluation.

Complexity is the source of much uncertainty. The complex, adaptive systems that comprise our world make the future unforeseeable.[10] Uncertainty presents a confounding problem to the strategist charged with shaping that future. Thus, strategists who ignore complexity depend heavily on the vagaries of chance. Conversely, those who appreciate and accommodate complexity, while not guaranteed success, improve their odds of achieving a favorable outcome.

According to Peter Checkland, complexity is best understood through a systems-thinking approach.[11] Checkland defined a system as "the idea of a set of elements connected together which form a whole . . . [with] properties which are properties of the whole, rather than properties of its component parts."[12] A system's complexity is primarily a function of three related variables: scale, interconnectedness, and interactivity. The latter two properties have external and internal dimensions. First, the size of a system factors into its complexity. Ceteris paribus, a system with many elements has the potential to be more complex than a simple system with few subcomponents. A system's internal and external connectivity also figures into its complexity. The degree to which a system is linked to its environment determines, in part, its ability to influence and be influenced by external factors. Open systems are connected and postured to import and export material, energy, or information.[13] For example, students of thermodynamics, biology, and sociology study open systems.[14] In contrast, closed systems are unconnected, unable to transfer internal matter to the outside, and vice versa; thus, they often behave mechanically.[15]

Additionally, a system's intrinsic connectedness determines the speed and extent to which inputs diffuse internally. In the realm of cybernetics, these connections take the form of feedback loops.[16] Charles Perrow explained that a highly coupled system is tightly interwoven.[17] Change in these systems, whether originating from within or without, promptly affects all subcomponents. Conversely, loosely coupled systems transfer material, energy, or information more slowly and less completely. An effect taken upon or within one part of this kind of system will not necessarily manifest itself elsewhere. Loosely coupled systems absorb shock more easily, while highly coupled systems find new equilibriums more rapidly.

Complexity is also a function of interactivity. As systems relate to other systems, they change one another. While it is obvious that only open systems experience external interaction, interactivity comes in degrees. Frequent interaction facilitates adaptation and makes a system more reflective of its environment.[18] Systems that infrequently interface with outside agents exhibit significant distinctness. Interactivity may also be endogenous. Systems with highly interactive subcomponents are dynamic, demonstrating vitality by generating change from within.[19] In contrast, systems with low levels of internal activity display less ebullience.

Our world is a complex, adaptive system of systems, massive in scale, highly interconnected, and exceptionally dynamic. No person, place, thing, or event is ever completely isolated.[20] Subsystems that frequently interact continually seek new equilibriums and bubble with the interactions of internal agents.[21] Our world includes innumerable combinations of open and closed, tightly coupled and loose, dynamic and static systems, as well as many in between. Additionally, it all exists in a temporal context of both past and future.[22] This amorphous and continually changing milieu is unknowable in its entirety. It is complex, inseparable, and alive.

Social Systems and Wicked Problems

Men and women comprise one of the most complex systems of our world—social systems. Human beings are self-conscious agents with a freedom of choice; this tendency infuses social systems with dynamism.[23] Checkland described social systems as "a mixture of a rational assembly of linked activities (a human activity system) and a set of relationships such as occur in a community (i.e., a natural system)."[24] According to Checkland, the relational component derives from man's social nature.[25] Studies of group dynamics reveal common behavioral patterns (e.g., formation of subgroups and alliances, development of tension and emotions, etc.).[26] These tendencies give social systems an element of predictability akin to many natural systems.

However, social systems are also malleable, peculiar, and surprising. A central feature is the presence of what Checkland calls human activity systems: "sets of human activities more or less consciously ordered in wholes as a result of some underlying purpose or mission."[27] That these systems are purposefully constructed and subject to redesign is not unique. The same is true of all designed systems.[28] What sets social systems apart is the self-determination of their course from within the system.[29]

Finally, social systems change as they respond to challenges. Internal or external stimuli that the system accommodates insufficiently will prompt adaptation. While problems induce change, the response of a social system is not automated. Redesign, like the original design, is elective; thus, how we understand the problem situation shapes consideration of its possible solutions.[30] Understanding is seldom straightforward because social problems are as complex as the systems that produce them.

Social problems reflect the complexity of their systems and are, in turn, also a source of complexity. Horst Rittel and Melvin Webber used the adjective "wicked" to describe most societal problems.[31] These problems are ill structured and lack objective evaluation criteria.[32] Hence, the character of a problem, or even its existence, is a matter of perspective. A further complication arises from society's plural nature. The presence of multiple groups, especially if in competition, makes a common viewpoint of the problem unlikely.[33] Consequently, there is seldom a definitive formulation of a social problem.[34] As Checkland notes, real-world problems reveal people wishing to take purposeful action; there can never be a single account of purposeful activity.[35]

Additionally, the interconnectedness of the system and multiple vantages of its agents increase the odds that the problem interrelates with other problems, as a symptom, a cause, or both.[36] The ever-changing nature of social systems makes each moment and problem unique, further complicating matters.[37] It also makes these problems unknowable in their entirety. Finally, because solutions are subjectively evaluated, each conceptualization of the problem creates multiple potential paths of action from which to choose. Strategists aiming to steer the system must account for the mixture of worldviews and agendas that present alternative and competing futures.

In sum, social systems present strategists with complex challenges. Successful strategy formulation requires an appreciation of the relevant systems—their scale, interconnectivity, and interactivity. Such strategies also need sufficient flexibility to accommodate the system's dynamism over time, including the shifting vantages of its multiple stakeholders. The multiple challenges of wicked problems, exposed by systems-thinking approaches, require holistic solutions. The ability to recognize and deal with the inherent complexity of strategy constitutes the virtue of design.

Design

Design is a multidisciplinary problem-solving approach. Brian Lawson asserted that designers "learn to understand problems that other people may find hard to describe and create good solutions for them."[38] Professional designers include architects, fashion designers, urban planners, engineers, and, increasingly, military officers.[39] What brings these diverse fields together is the complexity of their problems and the complexity-tolerant method they use to address them. Before specifically discussing the application of design to the profession of arms, we must first establish what design is and what designers do.

Design is a "highly complex mental process."[40] According to Lawson, it is a "negotiation between problem and solution through the activities of analysis, synthesis, and evaluation."[41] Analysis is the exploration of the system and problem; synthesis entails the "generation of solutions"; and evaluation involves the appraisal of suggested solutions against criteria identified during analysis.[42] Design moves back and forth between the problem and solution by cycling continually through its activities. Lawson contends that both the problem and solution emerge together from this nonlinear and ongoing process.[43]

Lawson disassembles the fundamental activities of design into five tasks: formulating, moving, representing, evaluating, and reflecting. In doing so, he constructs a sophisticated model that gives fidelity to both the process and the necessary skills of designers.[44] Formulating refers to the function of understanding and describing the problem.[45] It is roughly equivalent to the activity of analysis in the rudimentary model. As previously noted, this task can be complicated when the problem is unstructured, which is typical in social systems. Because the problem is part of its environment, formulation requires an understanding of the problem's context. Furthermore, how the problem is conceptualized influences all subsequent calculations.

Moving is similar to the notion of synthesis. The term suggests motion and involves making progress from understanding a problem to the generation of ideas and solutions.[46] Designers are solution focused and, like strategists, naturally drawn to this activity. However, developing solutions without some understanding of the problem can be misguided. Nevertheless, design is not a linear process and understanding is not a prerequisite for conjuring possible solutions. As part of the complex and adaptive system in which they exist, wicked problems are seldom fully knowable. Thus, uncertainty always exists. Formulating does not strictly precede moving, or the process would succumb to paralysis. Finally, as Karl Popper argued, hypotheses can only be refuted, never proven.[47] Dismissed and unsuccessful solutions sometimes help clarify our understanding of the problem. Ultimately, designers must use their imaginations to appreciate an uncertain situation and conjure creative solutions.

Representing entails depicting the relationship between a problem and its solution and may occur in many forms, including through language, computer models, and drawings. Lawson asserts that the most common medium is graphic.[48] Visual portrayals force designers to clarify their understanding of the situation and convey the perceived nature of the problem and solution. Because design is a collaborative effort, representation aids the process in two additional ways. First, portraits help foster a shared understanding among stakeholders who might otherwise talk past each other. Second, representations communicate the overarching concept of their endeavor to those responsible for implementing the solution.

Evaluating refers to the fact that designers regulate system actions by considering possible solutions against evaluation criteria.[49] For ill-structured problems, these criteria may be subjective and often lack consensus among relevant agents.[50] The identification of appraisal criteria occurs as the designer builds an understanding of the situation. Because complex systems are unknowable, designers must rely on their imaginations and their analytical skills to assess the evaluation criteria used for appraisals. Effective evaluations reveal the need to reconceive problems and solutions.

Finally, designers reflect on all aspects of their endeavor in a "continuous monitoring and learning process."[51] A good design process behaves like what Checkland labels an appreciative system.[52] According to him, the "interacting flux of events and ideas unfolding through time" is like a "two-stranded rope." The designer observes the flux, perceives reality, judges it, injects ideas, and catalyzes action that becomes part of the event stream.[53] Additionally, without an ultimate source of standards for appraisal (typical of social problems), the system's history becomes part of the basis for evaluation.[54] Learning occurs by reflecting on the system over time, and Donald Schön calls professionals with the skills to conduct such reflection "reflective practitioners."[55]

Vijay Govindarajan and Chris Trimble offer several recommendations to reflective practitioners that inform our understanding of design and will prove useful when juxtaposed with the practice of intelligence. First, instead of becoming overwhelmed with planning details, reflective practitioners should focus attention on a small number of critical unknowns that could have decisive consequences for organizational success or failure.[56] Second, analytical resources should concentrate on a plan's underlying assumptions rather than attempting to predict the future.[57] Third, when forecasting is necessary, it should take the form of trend analysis, without being forced to speculate on specific dates or details.[58] The authors also suggest periodic strategic reviews that account for rapidly changing environments without losing sight of historical lessons.[59] Finally, they advise measuring leading indicators that may anticipate the future rather than metrics that represent the existing environment.[60] Like Checkland, Govindarajan and Trimble conclude that because predicting the future of complex systems is impossible, learning from the past becomes an essential part of innovation.[61] Reflecting facilitates learning in an inventive design process.

In review, designers design the future by holistically and iteratively addressing the challenges of the present. According to Nigel Cross, designers "produce novel unexpected solutions, tolerate uncertainty, work with incomplete information, apply imaginative and constructive forethought to practical problems, and use drawings and other modeling media as a means of problem solving."[62] Restated using Lawson's model, they systemically conceptualize, creatively solve, artfully represent, incisively evaluate, and insightfully reflect upon complex challenges as they construct a better tomorrow. Good designers also bring the interpersonal, communication, and advocacy skills necessary to build some degree of consensus.

Conclusions

We live in a complex and adaptive system of systems that is enormous, in-tertwined, and amazingly alive. Systems thinking enables an appreciation of complex systems and a recognition of their continual change. It also assists the designers in identifying and solving the ill-structured problems that pro-pel social systems forward. Designers grapple with social challenges through a mental process by which they conceptualize the problem as a product of its environment, invent a solution, visualize the problem-solution relationship, appraise the solution, and learn through reflection.

Design is tolerant of complexity, which makes it useful for solving wicked problems. Its systems thinking approach engenders a holistic appreciation of the problem and solution, thereby decreasing the gap between understanding and reality. Its collaborative nature accounts for the pluralities of decision making in social systems, and its iterative character gives it the flexibility to accommodate the uncertainty and change inherent in complex problems. De-sign is well suited to address complex social challenges, including the most wicked of all—those that spark and are encountered in war.

Notes

1. Jomini, *Art of War*, 250, 306.

2. Clausewitz, *On War*, 100–12, 136.

3. Great-Quotes, "Napoleon Bonaparte Quotes," http://www.great-quotes.com/quotes/au-thor/Napoleon/Bonaparte/pg/5.

4. Campbell, "Psychological Test Profiles," 145–75; and Hughes, *Leadership*, 183.

5. Hughes, *Leadership*, 183.

6. Huntington, *Soldier and the State*, 59–60. He summarizes contemporary literature on the military mind that seems to agree with the psychological profile developed by Campbell and commented on by Hughes and Ulmer. Huntington wrote, "Military and civilian writers seem to agree that the military mind is disciplined, rigid, logical, scientific; it is not flexible, tolerant, intuitive, emotional."

7. Ulmer, "Military Leadership," 16–17.

8. Gray, "Stability Operations," 10.

9. This chapter leans heavily on the following scholarship regarding the theories of com-plexity, systems, and society: on complexity, see Waldrop, *Complexity*; and Barabasi, *Linked*; on systems see Checkland, *Systems Thinking, Systems Practice*; and on social problems see Rittel and Webber, "Dilemmas in a General Theory," 160–66.

10. Waldrop, *Complexity*, 145–47.

11. Checkland, *Systems Thinking, Systems Practice*, 3–7.

12. Ibid., 3.

13. Ibid., 82–83; and Bertalanffy, "Theory of Open Systems, 23–29."

14. Bertalanffy, "Theory of Open Systems," 25–27; Boulding, "General Systems Theory," 134; and Checkland, *Systems Thinking, Systems Practice*, 104–5.

15. Bertalanffy, "Theory of Open Systems," 23; and Checkland, *Systems Thinking, Systems Practice*, 104–5.

16. Wiener, *Human Use of Human Beings*, 33; and Brate, *Technomanifestos*, 14.

17. Perrow, *Normal Accidents*, 62–100.

18. See the discussion on fast transients in Boyd, "Patterns of Conflict," 5.

19. Checkland, *Systems Thinking, Systems Practice*, 74–82; and Waldrop, *Complexity*, 10–11.

20. In his 1974 work *Computer Lib*, the information revolutionary Theodor Holm Nelson described the interconnectedness of our world when he concluded, "Everything is deeply intertwingled." Quoted in Brate, *Technomanifestos*, 218.

21. Waldrop, *Complexity*, 11–12; and Barabasi, *Linked*, 6.

22. Neustadt and May, *Thinking in Time,* 247–70.

23. Checkland, *Systems Thinking, Systems Practice*, 116; Waldrop, *Complexity*, 11; and Barabasi, *Linked*, 6.

24. Checkland, *Systems Thinking, Systems Practice*, 121.

25. Ibid., 120.

26. Ibid.

27. Ibid., 111.

28. Ibid., 110, 118–19.

29. Ibid., A50.

30. Ibid., 154–55.

31. Rittel and Webber, "Dilemmas in a General Theory," 160.

32. Ibid.; and Checkland, *Systems Thinking, Systems Practice*, 155.

33. Rittel and Webber, "Dilemmas in a General Theory," 160.

34. Ibid.,161.

35. Checkland, *Systems Thinking, Systems Practice*, A54.

36. Rittel and Webber, "Dilemmas in a General Theory," 165.

37. Ibid., 163–64.

38. Lawson, *How Designers Think*, 5.

39. Ibid., 4–5. Lawson discusses the multidisciplinary nature and broad utility of design but does not address the applicability of design to the national security professional.

40. Ibid., 49.

41. Ibid.

42. Ibid., 37.

43. Ibid., 48.

44. Ibid., 291.

45. Ibid.

46. Ibid.

47. Popper, *Logic of Scientific Discovery*. This point is also made in Rittel and Webber, "Dilemmas in a General Theory," 166.

48. Lawson, *How Designers Think*, 291.

49. Ibid.

50. Rittel and Webber, "Dilemmas in a General Theory," 160.

51. Lawson, *How Designers Think*, 291.

52. Checkland, *Systems Thinking, Systems Practice*, A50–A52.

53. Ibid., A51.

54. Ibid., A52.

55. Schön, *Reflective Practitioner*, 291.

56. Govindarajan and Trimble, "Strategic Innovation," 70.

57. Ibid., 71. Refuting underlying assumptions disproves the theory or hypothesis that built the plan. See Popper, *Logic of Scientific Discovery*.

58. Govindarajan and Trimble, "Strategic Innovation," 72.

59. Ibid., 72–73.

60. Ibid., 73.

61. Ibid., 74.

62. Cross, "Nature and Nurture," 290.

Chapter 7

Operational Design

The first, the supreme, the most far-reaching act of judgment that the statesman and commander have to make is to establish by that test the kind of war on which they are embarking; neither mistaking it for, nor trying to turn it into, something that is alien to its nature. This is the first of all strategic questions and the most comprehensive.

—Carl von Clausewitz
On War

Now if the estimates made in the temple before hostilities indicate victory it is because calculations show one's strength to be superior to that of his enemy; if they indicate defeat, it is because calculations show that one is inferior. With many calculations, one can win; with few one cannot. How much less chance of victory has one who makes none at all! By this means I examine the situation and the outcome will be clearly apparent.

—Sun Tzu
The Art of War

Carl von Clausewitz asserted that the most crucial of all questions confronting statesmen and commanders is determining the kind of war a nation faces.[1] According to the Prussian theorist, two strategic imperatives comprise a war's nature: the political purpose, or what is to be achieved by the war; and the operational objective, or how the war is to be conducted.[2] Deciding the kind of war to wage—by determining its ends and ways—is the most comprehensive act of judgment and affects all subsequent calculations.[3]

Selecting the ends and ways is a complicated task compounded by the uncertainty and complexity endemic to the calculus of war. The complex problems that induce conflict are quintessentially "wicked." Furthermore, the international system in which wars occur, the societies that choose war, the armed forces that wage them, and war itself are complex, adaptive systems.[4] Wars, their components, and their contexts are nonlinear, systemic, iterative, human, and unpredictable.[5] Nevertheless, the challenge of complexity and intractability of wicked problems do not absolve the strategist of the responsibility to conceive of and build toward an improved future.[6] Sun Tzu, who understood the complexity of war, taught the value of a rigorous analytical process.[7] An understanding of the situation and outcome emerges from many calculations. This is also the essence of operational design.

This chapter considers operational design, beginning by outlining the concept's origin and background to circumscribe the subsequent evaluation. It defines the idea and distinguishes it from planning, explains the operational design method, and discusses the roles of the commander and the design team. The chapter concludes by summarizing the subject.

Operational design, like many good ideas, defies ownership. Furthermore, it is not static. Outlined below are key elements from a growing and increasingly varied scholarship on the concept. With few exceptions, this chapter does not repeat the basic features of design described previously. Rather, it concentrates on aspects of design that are peculiar to its practice in the armed forces.

The Origin and Background of Operational Design

Operational design uses design to solve the complex problems facing military commanders at the operational level of war. It represents an application of systems theory to operational art.[8] A brief description of operational design's origin and background is necessary before discussing its merits.

As previously noted, recognition of an operational level of war emerged in the Anglo-American military discourse in the 1980s.[9] Much had already been written to guide strategic-level decision making, and tactical problem-solving approaches seemed too linear to succeed at higher levels.[10] Practitioners in the intermediary tier—suspended between the strategic and tactical—sought rigorous, yet flexible intellectual approaches for their craft.[11] Thus, those who transferred design methods into the security discourse in the 1990s did so purposefully to fill what they perceived to be a cognitive void in operational art.[12] The association between design and the operational realm grew stronger as these concepts and their purveyors, especially retired Israeli brigadier general Shimon Naveh, found a home in receptive and influential American armed forces circles that were already exploring the operational level of war.[13]

Naveh's emphasis on systems theory and dialectic cognition in his 1997 book *In Pursuit of Military Excellence* gave a hint of what he later called systemic operational design.[14] For Naveh, systems thinking enabled operational art in three primary ways. First, conceptualizing their own forces as a complex, hierarchical system helped operational commanders understand their role as "steer[ing] the system towards the achievement of its [strategic] aim while forestalling the dangers of segregation and mechanization" of the system's specialized components.[15] Second, a systems analysis of oneself and one's enemy fostered an improved understanding of each side's strengths and weaknesses—a knowledge from which opportunity emerges.[16] Third, a systems approach facilitated learning. Naveh concluded that the "dialectic thinking" that can identify and match one's strength with an opponent's weakness was "the crucial cognitive quality required at the operational command echelons."[17]

Naveh illustrated his ideas with a historical analysis of post–World War I Soviet doctrine. He contended that Soviet theoreticians, seeking an alternative to costly annihilative strategies, conducted a thorough systems analysis that revealed an adversary's characteristics and faults.[18] From this new understanding arose the "Deep Battle" doctrine intended to induce operational shock in the enemy system without waging battles of destruction.[19] The Soviets, Naveh implied, had innovated using concepts that would later become systems theory.

King Solomon observed that "there is nothing new under the sun."[20] Operational design is no exception. Many of its elements are neither new to military theory nor original to operational design, as demonstrated by Naveh's retrospective analysis of early Soviet operational doctrine. Operational design hangs on a conceptual framework of four main ideas: systems, difference recognition, learning, and social creation (i.e., collaboration).[21] Critical and systems thinking, creative leadership and team-building, and iterative processes and organizational learning have long been part of strategy formulation and planning processes.

For example, with minimal conceptual stretching, many of these ideas are found in Clausewitz's *On War*. The interconnectedness of physical, mental, and moral factors; the center of gravity; and the preoccupation with unpredictability suggest the author's mastery of systems thinking.[22] The Prussian unambiguously believed that creative leadership in the form of genius provides an extraordinary advantage.[23] Furthermore, he contended repeatedly that the *zweikampf* that is war is "never an isolated act," "never a single short blow," and "never final." This indicates an appreciation for war's dynamic, iterative nature and the opportunity it presents to a commander willing to adapt and learn.[24] Many of operational design's concepts are not new but are repackaged in a fresh way, reminding military professionals that the military mind is most critical to success on the dynamic battlefield.

Because operational design is not planning, it does not replace existing planning processes.[25] Rather, it lives alongside and can be employed in concert with other approaches in ways that enrich the practice of operational art.

Gen James Mattis, then commander of the US Joint Forces Command, warned against the "over-proceduralization" of all planning processes and envisioned operational design as a way to invigorate "clear, careful thinking and creativity" within joint operation planning.[26]

While Mattis may have favored operational design over other constructs, the building of joint doctrine is a syncretic and evolving process.[27] Scholars have outlined how operational design and the military decision-making process can coexist.[28] Several have commented on the similarities between operational design and effects-based operations.[29] Additionally, a review of US joint doctrine indicates that the infiltration of operational design ideas increasingly influences joint planning, without necessarily displacing familiar constructs.[30] Operational design enhances existing joint planning processes.

Finally, operational design is not a static concept. Over time, it evolved beyond Naveh's original conception.[31] Furthermore, as it permeates operational discourse and doctrine, scholars interpret and apply its ideas in varying ways. They also pollinate operational design with concepts from other literature on operational art. While conceptual mutations are inevitable, they somewhat complicate this project's endeavor to consider operational design's relationship with intelligence. The following section describes this author's understanding of the practice of design.

Defining Operational Design

As asserted, operational design is the use of design to solve the complex problems facing military commanders at the operational level. The Joint Warfighting Center (JWFC), borrowing directly from US Army doctrine, defines it as "a methodology for applying critical and creative thinking to understand, visualize, and describe complex, ill-structured problems and develop approaches to solve them."[32] Because complex problems (and strategic guidance about them) are often obtuse and dynamic, operational design concentrates on problem identification. As John Schmitt explained, "The underlying premise of [operational design] is that if we understand a problem well enough, a solution to the problem becomes self-evident."[33]

Operational design's fixation with ascertaining the right problem distinguishes it from planning. For Schmitt, designing is problem setting and planning is problem solving.[34] The former involves "locating, identifying and formulating the problem, its underlying causes, structure and operative dynamics—in such a way that an approach to solving the problem emerges."[35]

Conversely, planning is "the process of devising, generally through the application of established procedures, a series of actions to be taken."[36]

Joint doctrine sees the distinction between designing and planning similarly: "Operational design is the conception and construction of the framework that underpins a joint operation plan and its subsequent execution."[37] Army doctrine, in contrast, considers designing part of planning, but its subtle differentiation is in consonance with joint doctrine. FM 5-0 states, "Planning consists of two separate, but closely related components: a conceptual component and a detailed component. The conceptual component is represented by the cognitive application of design. The detailed component translates broad concepts into a complete and practical plan."[38] Operational design is not planning; rather, they are two parts of the same whole.[39] Operational design precedes and occurs concurrently with planning.[40]

The Practice of Operational Design

So how is operational design performed?[41] US Army doctrine identifies three broad and concurrent steps: framing the environment, framing the problem, and considering operational approaches.[42] First, framing the operational environment involves "making sense of a complex reality."[43] A systems analysis, like that conducted to prepare the JIPOE, orders, groups, and characterizes the relevant actors and their relationships to foster an understanding of the situation.[44] The JIPOE includes a critical-factor analysis that identifies center(s) of gravity; critical capabilities, requirements, and vulnerabilities; and decisive points in the enemy system.[45] Environmental framing also entails the examination and synthesis of received guidance, including termination criteria, desired end state and conditions, objectives, and effects.[46] However, because there is no definitive formulation of an ill-structured problem, guidance can be nebulous or imprecise and requires careful consideration.[47]

Second, problem framing involves refining the environmental frame to isolate the root causes of the problem.[48] Understanding an operational problem requires an understanding of the context that produced it. Reciprocally, appreciation of an ill-structured problem illuminates the systems in which it resides. However, operational design appreciates the unknowable nature of both ill-structured problems and the complex, adaptive systems that comprise the operational environment. As Schmitt surmised, "Understanding a wicked problem is not a matter of capturing reality sufficiently correctly, but of constructing an interpretation that is sufficiently useful in dealing with reality."[49]

In framing the problem, the design team explores in finer detail the relationship between the desired outcome and the environmental and enemy systems. An appreciation of system tendencies as they relate to the desired outcomes is crucial. As this knowledge increases, designers identify the general aspects of the system that hold the potential to transform "existing conditions toward desired conditions."[50] The outcome of this step is "a narrative that explains the problem that must be addressed to achieve strategic aims."[51]

In the third step, designers develop the general operational approach. According to FM 5-0, this is "a broad conceptualization of the general actions that will produce the conditions that define the desired end state."[52] Designers must carefully consider the interconnectivity of the system upon which they propose to act and be mindful of the potentially unpredictable consequences of that action. As they think about potential solutions, designers deepen their understanding of the problem and environment.[53] Eventually, the operational approach describes a unique combination and synchronization of tasks and explains the mechanism that links those acts to the desired outcome.[54]

The JWFC adds two useful operational design steps to those described above.[55] The first is to "document the result."[56] Sometimes diagrams can concisely depict the design concept—the commander's visualization of the environment-problem-solution relationship. Army doctrine implores supplementing graphics with a narrative that explains the concept.[57] Keith Dickson suggests that designers portray the approach using logical lines of operation that graphically link the end state, objectives, conditions, effects, centers of gravity, decisive points, operational phases, and available means.[58] Regardless of the form it takes, the product should convey clearly the logic that will guide course-of-action development during the subsequent detailed planning stage.[59]

The final step of operational design is to "reframe as required."[60] According to JWFC's pamphlet on operational design, "Reframing is a process of revisiting earlier design hypotheses, conclusions, and decisions that underpin the current operational approach."[61] Incomplete understanding of complex adaptive systems and their wicked problems is probable and may only be appreciated through interaction over time. Interaction transforms systems in unexpected ways. During a campaign, the strategic aims may also change.[62] Continual assessment and reflection foster a deeper understanding of the environment, the problem, and the approach.[63] As often as necessary, the design process should restart to optimize effective action. The ability to reframe is evidence of organizational learning.

Leading Operational Design

Operational design is a commander-driven process.[64] Mattis, in his "Vision for a Joint Approach to Operational Design," felt the need to emphasize this point when he wrote, "To be absolutely clear, the commander actively leads the design effort."[65] As Schmitt argues, this does not mean the commander generates all of the ideas; rather, he is a direct participant in deciding who contributes to and learns from the process.[66] Ultimately, however, commanders own the operational concept they choose to implement, and it is their intuition that most directly contributes to and benefits from operational design.[67] The process assists them in understanding, visualizing, and describing complex problems and developing solutions.[68] Commanders enhance the quality of their design process. Their perspective is broader and more comprehensive than the staff's by virtue of experience and the extensive interaction with superiors, colleagues, subordinates, agency leaders, and multinational partners peculiar to their position.[69]

Commanders' wide-ranging relations also position them to exercise the collaborative leadership necessary for organizational learning.[70] Discourse is a critical and enabling feature of design with several benefits.[71] First, it is how commanders develop a shared understanding of the situation. As commanders move around the battlefield, they collect and impart information about the environment, the problem, and the operational approach.[72] Second, discourse fosters a shared commitment to possible solutions among stakeholders.[73] Third, discourse fosters innovation. It is egalitarian in its acceptance and distribution of ideas, which is especially helpful in the rigid hierarchy of a military organization. As Jack Kem concludes in *Design: Tools of the Trade*, "Design is a *team sport*. It helps to 'harvest the corporate intellect' of the commander, staff, superiors, and subordinates."[74] Finally, as the arena where narratives do battle, discourse hones concepts to describe reality more accurately and improve the commander's conceptualization of the situation.[75] Good commanders encourage the ongoing dialogue that enhances collaboration and learning.

The most regular contributors to the discourse will be the design team. Experts differ on the composition of the team; however, its central purpose is clear—to enhance the understanding of the commander. As such, commanders should take an active role in selecting their intellectual confidants. Teams are problem-centric entities that change over time as circumstances dictate.[76] While team size varies depending on the problem's nature and the resources available, teams are typically small groups.[77] Research suggests that a core team of five to six members is optimal.[78] Selection is based on expertise relative to the problem.[79] Critical and creative thinking skills are also precious attributes.[80] Ideal team composition should reflect a diversity of perspective that promotes the competitive intellectual environment necessary for dialectic discourse.[81] Army doctrine recommends that the team include key individuals from the planning staff who can ensure conceptual continuity when the design moves into detailed planning phases.[82] Finally, according to Schmitt, to the extent possible, design teams should consist of "key stake-holders with a compelling interest in the outcome of the situation."[83] Such people must live with the result of the design and will almost certainly participate in the recurring discourse.[84] In the end, regardless of composition, the design team aspires to assist the commander's holistic and simultaneous appreciation of the operational environment, problem, and potential solutions. In doing so, the team also develops its own awareness of the nature of the whole.

Conclusions

War's inherent problems are wicked, being a function of the interactions of complex systems. Determining the kind of war that looms or rages is the most essential of all judgments made by the statesman and commander. Operational design is a tool that assists such consequential assessment at the operational level of war.

Operational design is the use of design to solve the complex problems facing military commanders. It occurs in addition to planning and involves systems thinking, collaborative leadership, iterative decision making, and organizational learning to enrich operational art. Operational design places special emphasis on framing a problem to address its root causes. It entails simultaneous and reinforcing endeavors to understand the interconnected operational environment where the problem exists and potential action will occur; the problem itself, in all its complexity; and the most effective approach to solve the problem. This approach emerges from a growing appreciation of the situation.

Operational design is a commander-led process that relies on an inclusive and critical discourse to analyze ideas, synthesize concepts, facilitate learning, and foster a shared understanding of the environment and problem that drives the organization toward an effective solution. Design teams represent an extension of the commander's intellect. A team's purpose is not to think on behalf of the commander but to assist the commander's critical and creative conceptualization of the problem at hand.

Notes

1. Clausewitz, *On War*, 88–89.

2. Ibid., 579.

3. Ibid., 89, 579.

4. For a definition of complex adaptive systems (CAS), see Waldrop, *Complexity*, 11–12, 145–147. On international politics as a CAS, see Rosenau, "Many Damn Things Simultaneously," 32–43; and Friedman, *World Is Flat*. On societies as CAS, see Waldrop, *Complexity*; and Checkland, *Systems Thinking, Systems Practice*, 120–21. On armed forces as CAS, see Abb, "A Living Military System." On war as a CAS, see Schmitt, "Command and (Out of) Control," 99–111.

5. Beyerchen, "Clausewitz, Nonlinearity," 59–90.

6. For more on wicked problems, see Rittel and Webber, "Dilemmas in a General Theory," 160–66.

7. Sun Tzu, *Illustrated Art of War*, 103.

8. Sorrells, Downing, Blakesley, Pendall, Walk, and Wallwork, "Systemic Operational Design," 15.

9. Luttwak, "Operational Level of War," 61–79; and Simpkin, *Deep Battle*, x.

10. Davison, "Systemic Operational Design (SOD)," 3–16. Davison argues that both the joint operation planning and execution system and military decision-making process encouraged linear and mechanistic approaches to operational planning.

11. Effects-based operations provide one example of a systemic approach to operational art that emerged in the 1990s. See Deptula, *Effects-Based Operations*; and the Joint Warfighting Center (JWFC), *Operational Implications of Effects-Based Operations*.

12. Naveh, *In Pursuit of Military Excellence*, 4; and Sorrells, Downing, Blakesley, Pendall, Walk, and Wallwork, "Systemic Operational Design," 8. The Anglo-American discourse that recognized an operational level of war in the 1980s also included the Israeli defense and security apparatus. Israeli Defense Forces (IDF) borrowed heavily from American military doctrine, and their military theorists contributed extensively to the English-speaking debate. Clearly, the most relevant example for this project is that the founders of systemic operational design (the predecessor of operational design) were veterans of the IDF and/or employees of the IDF-sponsored Operational Theory Research Institute (OTRI).

13. Perhaps most influential was the US Army's School of Advanced Military Studies, which began a relationship with Naveh in the mid-1990s and later (2005) hired him and others associated with OTRI as faculty members and student advisors. See Ryan, *Art of Design*, 1–3.

14. Systemic operational design will be referred to as SOD.

15. Naveh, *In Pursuit of Military Excellence*, 7.

16. Ibid., 16.

17. Ibid., 306.

18. Ibid., 16.

19. Ibid. For a helpful expansion on how complexity theory informs the concept of operational shock, see Blakesley, "Operational Shock." For a critique of Naveh's analysis, see Vego, "Case against Systemic Operational Design," 69–75. Vego accuses Naveh of "falsely reinterpret[ing] the early Soviet writings on operational art in terms of [General Systems Theory]" to provide SOD an operational pedigree.

20. Eccles. 1:9.

21. Ryan, *Art of Design*, 41–58.

22. Beyerchen, "Clausewitz, Nonlinearity," 66–72. Another example of an operational approach in which systems theory plays an obvious role is effects-based operations (EBO). Some scholars trace EBO's systems thinking beyond the US Army's Air Corps Tactical School, where, between the twentieth century's world wars, industrial web theory informed the thinking of strategic bombing pioneers. See Fadok, "John Boyd and John Warden"; and Meilinger, "History of Effects-Based Air Operations," 139–68. Some proponents of SOD distinguish its use of systems thinking about an opponent from that of EBO by claiming the former conceives of the enemy as an open system and the latter as a closed system. See, for example, Davison, "Systemic Operational Design (SOD)," 17–52; and Vego, "Case against Systemic Operational Design," 73–74. The present author assesses that users of EBO have mistakenly visualized opponents as closed systems in the past but that doing so was a misapplication of the approach rather than its inherent inflexibility.

23. Clausewitz, *On War*, 100–12.

24. Ibid., 78–79.

25. Schmitt, "Systemic Concept for Operational Design."

26. Mattis, "Vision for a Joint Approach."

27. Ibid.; and Mattis, "USJFCOM Commander's Guidance," 18–25; on the nature of doctrine integration, see Posen, *Sources of Military Doctrine*, 41–54.

28. For example, see Davison, "Systemic Operational Design (SOD)."

29. For example, see McGlade, "Effects-Based Operations." In Davison, "Systemic Operational Design (SOD)," the author's comparison of SOD and EBO reveals both significant similarity and real difference between the two constructs. In Vego, "Case against Systemic Operational Design," the author also highlights similarities and differences between SOD and EBO. For an argument on the enduring utility of EBO, see Ruby, "Effects-Based Operations," 26–35.

30. For example, both operational design and effects are represented in JP 5-0, *Joint Operation Planning*, xiii; and JP 3-0, *Joint Operations*. JP 5-0 states, "Joint operation planning blends two complementary processes. The first is the joint operation planning process; the second process is operational design."

31. Elkus and Burke, "Operational Design, 147–48."

32. JWFC, *Design in Military Operations*, 4; and FM 5-0, *Operations Process*, 3–1.

33. Schmitt, "Systemic Concept for Operational Design," 3, 5–7.

34. Ibid., 3; and Sorrells, Downing, Blakesley, Pendall, Walk, and Wallwork, "Systemic Operational Design," 15.

35. Schmitt, "Systemic Concept for Operational Design," 6.

36. Ibid.

37. JP 5-0, *Joint Operation Planning*, IV-2.

38. FM 5-0, *Operations Process*, 3–1.

39. JWFC, *Design in Military Operations*, 32.

40. An illustration of this distinction that may be familiar to Airmen is the difference between the functions of the strategy and plans divisions in an air and space operations center. The former designs the way airpower will be employed, while the latter's detailed planning—which produces the joint integrated prioritized targeting list and master air attack plan—puts flesh on the construct's skeleton. See Air Force Tactics, Techniques and Procedures 3-3AOC, *Operational Employment–Air and Space Operations Center*.

41. Lawson, *How Designers Think*, 291. Lawson identified five design activities: formulating, moving, representing, evaluating, and reflecting.

42. FM 5-0, *Operations Process*, 3-7; John Schmitt offers a more involved seven-step design process in Schmitt, "Systemic Concept for Operational Design," 20–23. The more simple US Army doctrinal approach suffices for this project.

43. FM 5-0, *Operations Process*, 3-8.

44. JP 2-01.3, *Joint Intelligence Preparation*.

45. Ibid., II-65–67; JP 5-0, *Joint Operation Planning*, IV-8–15; and Reilly, *Operational Design*, 25–32.

46. JP 5-0, *Joint Operation Planning*, IV-4–8; and FM 5-0, *Operations Process*, 3-9.

47. Rittel and Webber, "Dilemmas in a General Theory," 161.

48. FM 5-0, *Operations Process*, 3-10.

49. Schmitt, "Systemic Concept for Operational Design," 10.

50. FM 5-0, *Operations Process*, 3-10–11.

51. US Army Training and Doctrine Command (TRADOC) Pamphlet 525-5-500, *Commander's Appreciation and Campaign Design*, 24.

52. FM 5-0, *Operations Process*, 3-11.

53. Schmitt, "Systemic Concept for Operational Design," 10.

54. FM 5-0, *Operations Process*, 3-11.

55. JWFC, *Design in Military Operations*, 4.

56. Ibid., 15–16.

57. FM 5-0, *Operations Process*, 3-12.

58. Ibid., 3-11; and Dickson, *Operational Design*.

59. FM 5-0, *Operations Process*, 3-11.

60. JWFC, *Design in Military Operations*, 4.

61. Ibid., 16.

62. TRADOC, *Commander's Appreciation and Campaign Design*, 17.

63. Ryan, *Art of Design*, 109, 116.

64. This is more axiomatic of command than it is design.

65. Mattis, "Vision for a Joint Approach," 6.

66. Schmitt, "Systemic Concept for Operational Design," 22–23.

67. Ibid., 22; and Mattis, "USJFCOM Commander's Guidance," 6.

68. FM 5-0, *Operations Process*, v.

69. Mattis, "USJFCOM Commander's Guidance," 6.

70. Kem, *Design*, 27–30.

71. DiPasquale, "Discourse in Systemic Operational Design." DiPasquale argues that a single discourse is comprised of multiple simultaneous discourses that each serves unique functions. For example, there may be a metadiscourse that builds consensus, while another structures the process, and another builds the design narrative.

72. Battlefield circulation is an important part of the US Army's battle command concept. For more on both ideas, see FM 3-0, *Operations*. For a discussion on the relationship between design and battle command, see Kem, *Design*; and McHenry, "Battle Command."

73. Schmitt, "Systemic Concept for Operational Design," 19; and Conklin, *Dialogue Mapping*, 29.

74. Kem, *Design*, 63.

75. Ryan, *Art of Design*, 77.

76. FM 5-0, *Operations Process*, 3-6.

77. Schmitt, "Systemic Concept for Operational Design," 22; and Ryan, *Art of Design*, 20.

78. Ryan, *Art of Design*, 20; and Hammerstrom, "Size Matters, 2."

79. FM 5-0, *Operations Process*, 3-6.

80. Stephen Wright, "A Conversation on the Composition of Design Teams," interview by the author, 8 April 2011.

81. Schmitt, "Systemic Concept for Operational Design," 22.

82. FM 5-0, *Operations Process*, 3-6.

83. Schmitt, "Systemic Concept for Operational Design," 22.

84. Ibid.

Chapter 8

Operational Design in the Malayan Emergency

The policy of HM Government in the United Kingdom is that Malaya should in due course become a fully self-governing nation. HM Government confidently hope that that nation will be within the British Commonwealth. . . . To achieve a United Malayan nation there must be a common form of citizenship for all who regard the Federation or any part of it as their real home and the object of their loyalty. It will be your duty to guide the peoples of Malaya toward the attainment of these objectives and to promote such political progress of the country as will, without prejudicing the campaign against terrorists, further our democratic aims in Malaya.

> —Directive to General Templer
> from Mr. Lyttelton
> 7 February 1952

In December 1951, after conducting a fact-finding tour of Malaya, Oliver Lyttelton, the British secretary of state for the colonies, described the Malayan Emergency as follows:

> The situation was far worse than I had imagined: it was appalling. . . . I have never seen such a tangle as that presented by the Government of Malaya. . . . There was divided and often opposed control at the top. . . . The two authorities [civil and military] were apparently co-equal, neither could overrule the other outside his own sphere. But what was each sphere? The frontiers between their responsibilities had not been clearly defined, indeed they were indefinable, because no line could be drawn to show where politics, civil administration, police action, administration of justice and the like end, and where para-military or military operations begin. The civil administration moved at a leisurely pace. . . . The police itself was divided by a great schism between the Commissioner of Police and the Head of the Special Branch. Intelligence was scanty and uncoordinated between the military and the civil authorities. . . . Morale amongst planters, tin miners, and amongst Chinese loyalists and Malays, was at its lowest. The grip of terrorists was tightening, and the feelings of the loyalists could be summed up in one word, despair.[1]

In the vernacular of operational design, Malaya posed a wicked problem.[2] The Malayan Emergency provides an intelligence success story and also offers an example of successful operational design.

This chapter reconsiders the Malayan Emergency through the lens of operational design. It begins by evaluating the development of Lt Gen Sir Harold Briggs's understanding that led to his crucial reframing of the situation from a terrorism threat to a governance challenge. Next, it highlights Briggs's collaborative leadership as he assembled the eventually successful operational approach. It then examines Gen Sir Gerald Templer's opportunity to reframe the problem, his leadership through discourse, and his selection of a core design team that included his director of intelligence. The chapter concludes that the Malayan Emergency demonstrated many key elements of operational design, including its close relationship with intelligence.

Before proceeding, it is necessary to comment briefly on this chapter's method. Imposing a contemporary construct, such as operational design, on past events risks committing a *post hoc ergo propter hoc* logical fallacy. While this analytical danger neither negates the utility of a retrospective evaluation nor invalidates its inferences, it does make the following argument suggestive rather than authoritative. Nevertheless, there is value in considering whether and how the events of the Malayan Emergency resemble the operational design process for this project's forthcoming synthesis of insights from operational intelligence and operational design.

Briggs's Reframing of the Environment and the Problem

While Templer received credit for the vigorous leadership that broke the insurgency, Briggs's concept provided the blueprint for victory. Briggs's approach proved successful because it addressed the right problem. His plan maintained elements of the existing counterterrorism strategy that sought to defeat the MCP.[3] However, he understood that this effort was insufficient; terrorism was only a symptom of the emergency's root cause.

Briggs's analysis reframed the situation. As he better understood the operational environment, he recognized the problem as being the political disenfranchisement of the Chinese squatters. A prominent environmental factor was that British policy sought the eventual peaceful decolonization of a stable Malaya within its economic sphere of influence.[4] Achieving this end was impossible as long as the insurgency raged on and improbable without reconciling the demographic fissures within Malayan society. Furthermore, it would require effective self-administration. From his appreciation of both the environment and problem emerged an operational approach. Briggs concluded that the people were the center of gravity of both the insurgency and the Malayan government, and he refocused the government's energy on an indirect counter to the insurgency—isolating the MCP through good governance.[5] The use of force would purchase the space and time required for his plan to work.

How Briggs's winning plan came into being remains somewhat unclear.[6] Nevertheless, what we know about his development of understanding and an operational approach is instructive. He sought insight from three primary sources. First, while the intelligence system remained imperfect, after two years of counterinsurgency experience in Malaya, its appreciation of the environment appears to have informed Briggs's assessment.[7] Second, in a sort of battlefield circulation, Briggs met with a multitude of civilian, military, and business leaders throughout the country upon arriving in Malaya, each of whom added to his understanding of the challenge.[8]

Third, Briggs conducted his own analysis, using his extensive experience and impeccable judgment.[9] He had served in the British army since 1914, spending most of his time in Asia.[10] Thus, Briggs was familiar, at least in part, with the cultures and mind sets of the Asians with whom he worked.[11] His service in Burma also brought a familiarity with jungle warfare and civil administration during an era of decolonization and rising nationalism.[12]

As well, Briggs had a reputation for being imaginative and incisive.[13] Field Marshal William Slim, his commander in Burma, wrote admiringly of him: "I know of few commanders who made as many immediate and critical decisions on every step of the ladder of promotion, and I know of none who made so few mistakes."[14] Ultimately, Briggs proved to be an exceptional analyst who was more than capable of appreciating the complexities of the communist insurgency in Malaya.

Briggs's Development of an Operational Approach

The operational approach that became Briggs's eponymous plan emerged from his conceptualization of the environment and problem. However, the solution, like the analysis, was not his alone; rather, it was the product of a collaborative process. Counterinsurgency was familiar to the British colonial experience, as were population control measures used to separate guerrillas from their support. For example, Briggs and his colleagues would have known about Lord Horatio Kitchener's resettlement of civilians between 1900 and 1902 during the Second Boer War.[15]

Furthermore, it is likely that High Commissioner Sir Henry Gurney, with two years experience in Malaya, had concrete ideas on how to wage the counterinsurgency. Gurney had already begun working to resettle Chinese squatters before Briggs arrived.[16] One author attributed to Gurney the perceptive notion that squatter resettlement would simultaneously integrate Malayan society and disrupt MCP support.[17] Additionally, one of Gurney's key assistants and later a close advisor to Briggs, the Malayan civil servant Robert Thompson, drafted the Briggs Plan after numerous meetings with the director of operations and his military staff officers.[18] To single out Gurney or Thompson as the source of the emergency's successful counterinsurgency concepts is as misguided as it is to credit Briggs alone. The operational approach resulted from a process of developing a shared understanding of the environment, the problem, and the potential solutions.

Nevertheless, the advent of the Briggs Plan demonstrated the leadership and incisiveness of the man for whom it was named.[19] Briggs led the design process, supplementing others' assessments with his own analysis, engaging numerous contributors to the discourse, incorporating various inputs into the concept, and all along relying on his own experience and judgment. He assumed ownership of his design and gained support for it from the British Defence Coordination Committee, Far East, in May 1950, and from the Cabinet Malaya Committee, in July.[20] He was also accountable for carrying it out. In the end, Briggs was the design's chief architect, and the Briggs Plan became a worthy legacy.

Templer and Operational Design

Three aspects of Templer's tenure round out the Malayan Emergency's illustration of operational design. One elucidates reframing; another emphasizes discourse; and the third provides an example of design-team composition. A change of command is a natural opportunity to reassess a situation and reframe if required. John Cloake argued, in *Templer: Tiger of Malaya*, that the general's first and primary concern upon taking command was to "get the priorities right."[21] Templer received Lyttelton's strategic guidance shortly before arriving in Malaya in February 1952.[22] Once there, Templer began an exhaustive review to develop his own awareness of the situation. In the end, his analysis of the environment, of the problem, and of the optimal operational approach aligned closely with that of his predecessor. Templer found no need to reframe the situation and endorsed the Briggs Plan as his operational approach for solving the emergency.[23]

Templer developed his understanding of the Malayan Emergency in part through discourse.[24] Within a week of his arrival, he hosted all of the British advisors in the country and their wives, talking with them "into the small hours" of the night.[25] He constantly toured Malaya and engaged his superiors, staff, subordinate commanders and forces, leaders of the Malayan and Chinese communities, and the people of Malaya in an ongoing conversation.[26] One police commandant recalled, "Then [Templer] went on to say that he would ask advice from his staff and all those concerned before making plans. That was the time to offer advice, to put forward plans—however different or controversial, and to criticise. All would be listened to and taken into account."[27] Templer cast his net wide for ideas and welcomed the participation of even midlevel officials in this discourse.

The composition of Templer's core design team was also instrumental to his success. As the dual-hatted high commissioner and director of operations, Templer moved in many circles and participated in multiple councils and committees. However, he relied on the Director of Operations Committee that met three times weekly to help in the oversight of operations.[28] This committee assisted his critical thinking and development of ideas. Templer presided over the committee and populated it with key members of his organization who were also responsible for implementing the concepts he approved. They included his deputy director of operations, chief secretary, secretary for defence, director of intelligence, ground operations commander, air operations commander, and chief of police.[29] Guy Madoc, appointed director of intelligence in 1954, later highlighted the inclusion of the intelligence director on the operations committee as one of Templer's major innovations. He claimed, "I heard many times this was the first instance [in the history of the British Empire] of the absolute importance of Intelligence being given full recognition. I know that it was true of Malaya."[30]

Conclusion

This inferential analysis of the Malayan Emergency using the contemporary rubric of operational design found that elements of operational design are retrospectively evident. Collaborative leadership and discourse played an important role assisting in the development of understanding for both Briggs and Templer. Briggs's appreciation of the complex operational environment and the wicked problem represented by the emergency caused him to reframe the challenge as one of good governance. He concluded that the existing counterterrorism strategy was insufficient because it did not address the root problem of Chinese disenfranchisement. From his enhanced understanding of the environment and the problem emerged an operational approach that became the successful Briggs Plan.

Templer developed his own appreciation of the situation upon his arrival in Malaya and determined that reframing was unnecessary. His understanding of the environment, the problem, and the optimal operational approach was consistent with that of his predecessor. Despite the fact that reframing was not required, Templer's extensive consultations and intense mental activity leading to this conclusion were quite valuable because they gave him a deep conviction in the soundness of the overall approach and an awareness of the variations with which it would have to be implemented. He executed the Briggs Plan with vigor and innovation, surrounding himself with a core design team comprised of key stakeholders within his command, including his director of intelligence.

Notes

1. Lyttelton, *Memoirs of Lord Chandos*, 366–67; and Coates, *Suppressing Insurgency*, 110–11.

2. Rittel and Webber, "Dilemmas in a General Theory," 160–66.

3. Bennett, "'A Very Salutary Effect,'" 417.

4. Stockwell, "British Imperial Policy," 68–87; and Stockwell, "Insurgency and Decolonisation," 71–81.

5. CAB 21/1681, MAL C(50)23, appendix, "Federation Plan for the Elimination of the Communist Organization and Armed Forces in Malaya" (the Briggs Plan): Report by COS for Cabinet Malaya Committee, 24 May 1950, in Stockwell, *British Documents*, 216–21; Short, "Communism and the Emergency," 155; Clutterbuck, *Long Long War*, 57; and Coates, *Suppressing Insurgency*, 82.

6. The author attributes the lack of scholarship on the advent of the Briggs Plan to two main factors. First, much of the early literature on Malaya emphasizes the role of leadership in the emergency's success and focuses on Templer. Briggs's positive contributions were largely obscured by the grave indicators that punctuated his command's conclusion, including high-water marks on most security metrics and the assassination of Gurney. Second, his premature death as well as the passing of other key principals compounded the initial relative lack of interest in Briggs. These premature losses deprived historians of the opportunity to record their narratives as fully as was done with survivors such as Templer. Briggs died in 1952, just months after retiring from Malaya, leaving no papers. Gurney was assassinated in October 1951, and Gent, Gurney's predecessor, died in an aircraft crash in July 1948 during his return to England from Malaya.

7. See the argument made in chapter 5 of this project.

8. Coates, *Suppressing Insurgency*, 81–82.

9. Short, "Communism and the Emergency," 155.

10. Clutterbuck, *Long Long War*, 57; and Coates, *Suppressing Insurgency*, 81.

11. Coates, *Suppressing Insurgency*, 81.

12. Ibid.

13. Clutterbuck, *Long Long War*, 57.

14. Slim, *Defeat into Victory*, 145.

15. Parkenham, *Boer War*, 522.

16. Barber, *War of the Running Dogs*, 61–71, 93–100.

17. Ibid.

18. Ibid., 96–97.

19. The Briggs Plan seems to be an example of the Matthew effect and its corollary, Stigler's law of eponymy, which state that a combination of sociological factors result in the regular misattribution of credit for great accomplishments: "No scientific discovery is named after its original discoverer." While the concepts inherent in the Briggs Plan may not have belonged to Briggs alone, he did much to turn the concepts into reality. Briggs presented the plan as the "Federation plan for the elimination of the communist organization and armed forces in Malaya." However, his advocacy—and the plan's unwieldy official title—probably resulted in the association of Briggs with the plan. The shortened title naturally assumed his name. According to John Coates, the *Straits Times* first called it the "Briggs War Plan" on 12 June 1950 and later the "Briggs Plan" on 6 August. See note 22 in Coates, *Suppressing Insurgency*, 102; see comment in Stockwell, *British Documents*, 216. On the Matthew effect, see Merton, "Matthew Effect in Science," 56–63. On Stigler's law, see Gieryn, *Science and Social Structure*, 147–57.

20. Stockwell, *British Documents*, 216; and Coates, *Suppressing Insurgency*, 82.

21. Cloake, *Templer*, 227.

22. Lyttelton, "Directive Addressed to General Templer by Secretary of State for the Colonies, published 7 February 1952," in Coates, *Suppressing Insurgency*, 205–06.

23. Coates, *Suppressing Insurgency*, 118.

24. Like Briggs, Templer probably relied on a combination of intelligence, intuition, and discourse to develop his understanding. Chapter 5 discussed the improving quality of analysis. Additionally, Templer's qualifications and intellect were exceptional. His use of discourse, however, deserves emphasis in this chapter. See Cloake, *Templer*, for a thorough account of the man.

25. Ibid., 213.

26. Coates, *Suppressing Insurgency*, 116.

27. Cloake, *Templer*, 213.

28. CO 1022/60, no 3, [Reorganisation of Government]: Inward Telegram No 268 from Sir G Templer to Mr Lyttelton On New Measures, 28 Feb 1952, in Stockwell, *British Documents*, 375.

29. Ibid.

30. Short, *Communist Insurrection in Malaya*, 360; and Nagl, *Learning to Eat Soup*, 92. For more on Guy Madoc, see Cloake, *Templer*, 231–35.

Chapter 9

A Synthesis of Operational Intelligence and Operational Design

There are some things that you know to be true, and others that you know to be false; yet despite this extensive knowledge that you have, there remain many things whose truth or falsity is not known to you. We say that you are uncertain about them. You are uncertain to varying degrees, about everything in the future; much of the past is hidden from you; and there is a lot of the present about which you do not have full information. Uncertainty is everywhere and you cannot escape from it.

—Dennis Lindley
Understanding Uncertainty

What is called "foreknowledge" cannot be elicited from spirits, nor from gods, nor by analogy with past events, nor from calculations. It must be obtained from men who know the enemy situation.

—Sun Tzu
The Art of War

Uncertainty is everywhere; it is inescapable, especially in war.[1] Efforts to mitigate it represent the conceptual bridge connecting operational intelligence and operational design. In some respects, the latter exists because of the former's failure to vanquish uncertainty. Uncertainty drove commanders to build sophisticated intelligence organizations to dispel the fog of war; it also pushed them toward elaborate cognitive processes to manage that fog. Both intelligence and design are extensions of the operational-level commander's mind. Intelligence aims to ask and answer the right questions; design seeks to identify and solve the right problems. Intelligence collects and analyzes information to build understanding of a complex situation; design translates a tenuous understanding into an approach for achieving operational aims and strategic ends. Intelligence strives to make sense of past and current circumstances to inform future action; design endeavors to mold the future based on what is learned from the past and known about the present. Without uncertainty, there would be no need for intelligence or design; because of uncertainty, intelligence and design are two sides of the same coin.

The Chinese theorist Sun Tzu asserted that, to the extent it is possible, certainty is "obtained from men who know the enemy situation."[2] While this maxim referred to the ability of effective spies to know the enemy's immediate intent, it also describes the ability of effective designers to shape a preferred future. This chapter synthesizes insights from the previous chapters to answer the research question: How should the practice of operational intelligence be influenced by the concepts of operational design?

Five significant insights for the practice of intelligence at the operational level of war emerge from the synthesis of operational intelligence and operational design. The chapter begins by evaluating the tension within operational intelligence between the strategic and tactical perspectives of war. Second, it assesses the crucial function of intelligence in organizational learning during wartime. It then appraises the priceless benefit of collaboration in the practice of operational intelligence. Next, it considers briefly what most designers expect from intelligence—the joint intelligence preparation of the operational environment. The last insight involves the central role of the intelligence advisor at the operational level of war. The chapter concludes that a closer integration of the complementary activities of operational intelligence and operational design, under the command of a flexible-minded and collaborative leader, is a promising construct for the rich and successful practice of operational art.

Balancing the Strategic and Tactical
of Operational Intelligence

The most important lesson operational design offers to the practice of operational intelligence is a reminder of the primacy of strategic over tactical matters. A premise of operational design is that to be effective a solution must address the correct problem. Operational design concentrates on understanding strategic and operational problems and evaluating the operational mechanism used to achieve desired strategic outcomes and operational objectives. This unceasing effort lifts the commander's gaze away from tactical concerns and toward issues that closely affect strategy. Strategy and tactics are both essential. Strategy without tactics is toothless; tactics without strategy lacks purpose.[3] Nevertheless, operational design's continuous quest to discern and tackle the correct problem reminds us that the scale favors strategy.

Operational design continually seeks to identify and address the root causes of a complex problem. An operational approach that quells a problem's symptoms without contributing to the solution of its causes risks never achieving the strategic objective, regardless of how exceptional its tactical employment.[4] Allan R. Millett and Williamson Murray, editors of and contributors to the landmark multivolume *Military Effectiveness*, made this argument of strategy over tactics. They sounded the following warning in an article that summarized their monumental work: "No amount of operational [or tactical] virtuosity . . . redeemed fundamental flaws in political judgment. . . . This is because it is more important to make correct decisions at the political and strategic level than it is at the operational or tactical level. Mistakes in operations and tactics can be corrected [admittedly at a cost]. But, political and strategic mistakes live forever."[5]

Similarly, as John Cushman concluded in his chapter of *Military Effectiveness,* entitled "Challenge and Response at the Operational and Tactical Levels, 1914–45," the insight that produces good strategy allows even those who bungle its prosecution a chance of success, while first-rate tactical performance alone is insufficient.[6] Operational design is the relentless pursuit of such strategic insight, which is of paramount importance.

From the vantage of operational design, the purpose of operational intelligence is to spark insight in the commander's mind that aids conceptualization of the military operation or the campaign leading to the strategic goal. Operational intelligence considers both strategy and tactics as it informs their alignment. It is pulled between both poles. Because tactical intelligence is a powerful force multiplier, it has an obvious and, at times, distracting magnetism. However, it is unwise to perform intelligence activities that facilitate tactics without first satisfying requirements at the operational level's higher end. As Thomas Mahnken wrote, "Technological proficiency is no substitute for strategic acuity."[7] Thus, the lesson for the intelligence professional at the operational level of war is about balance.

Today, operational-level organizations control a number of ISR capabilities, traditional and otherwise, that facilitate tactical employment. For example, the overwatch of friendly ground forces is a common mission for airborne platforms in Afghanistan and Iraq.[8] Modern airpower's "kill chain"—its capacity to find, fix, track, target, engage, and assess—requires a substantial commitment of collection and analytical resources for a single sortie.[9] Both overwatch and the "kill chain" are two examples of the indispensable contributions by ISR assets to the employment of force. Operational-level commanders and their intelligence advisors are correct to enable action by augmenting the ISR capabilities organic to lower echelon forces; however, intelligence support to tactics should seldom come at the expense of the operation or the campaign.

The most essential charge of operational intelligence is to assist the commander's understanding of the environment and the problem. The operational approach emerges from this understanding. The questions and efforts that assess the operational-level situation seldom coincide with those that facilitate tactical action. The intelligence director must ensure the aggressive, continual collection and analysis of the commander's PIR to make sense of the complex, dynamic combinations of objective and subjective factors that comprise the operational environment and the operational problem. In an ideal situation, the intelligence advisor supports all customers sufficiently. When a choice must be made, the long-term ISR balance should favor the operational-level commander over the tactical unit.

The Malayan Emergency provides a supportive historical example as a final point on the relative importance of strategy and tactics to the operational-level commander and the intelligence apparatus. The emergency's successful turning hinged on Lt Gen Sir Harold Briggs's reframing of the situation away from an MCP–centric problem that warranted a counterterrorism response to a population-centric challenge that required a counterinsurgency approach based chiefly on political inclusion and improved governance. Had the Briggs Plan not reallocated the energy and resources of the British government as it did, it seems unlikely that MCP support would have wilted.

In Malaya, tactical intelligence depended on assistance from the population. While intelligence support to tactical units was almost nonexistent during the prosecution of the counterterrorism strategy, after the Briggs Plan took effect, SB produced increasingly accurate assessments that enabled the methodic elimination of communist insurgents. Thus, the most important intelligence products of the Malayan Emergency were those that helped Briggs and Gen Sir Gerald Templer accurately frame the situation and arrive at their successful operational approach.

Operational Intelligence and Organizational Learning

A related lesson operational design offers to the practice of operational intelligence concerns the role of intelligence in organizational learning. Once Briggs correctly framed the Malayan Emergency, the probability of success improved significantly. Operational design reminds us that operational intelligence must foremost assess the operational-level situation to aid the commander's understanding.

Stephen R. Rosen averred that wartime learning and innovation are un-common.[10] A brief consideration of Rosen's argument and his perspective on intelligence helps illuminate how operational intelligence aids organizational learning. Rosen asserted that armed forces routinely measure their operational performance but are only capable of gauging established strategic measures of effectiveness for which feedback loops already exist.[11] His point is worth restating in full here:

> When military innovation is required in wartime, however, it is because an inappropriate strategic goal is being pursued, or because the relationship between military operations and that goal has been misunderstood. The old ways of war are employed, but no matter how well, the war is not being won. A new strategic goal must be selected and a new relationship between military operations and that goal must be defined. Until that happens, information will be collected that is relevant to the old goals and relations, and there is no reason to suppose that this information will suggest new, alternative ways of winning the war. Until the strategic measure of effectiveness has been redefined, organizational learning relevant to innovation cannot take place.[12]

Rosen's argument about the circumstances that require wartime innovation has merit and highlights an important potential contribution of intelligence at the operational level of war. Evaluating the strategic goal and the relationship between military operations and that goal is a purpose of intelligence assessments and of the environmental framing step in the operational design process. Rosen dismissed intelligence—the determination of "the number and location of enemy units"—as an inadequate mechanism for learning and improving organizational performance in wartime.[13] However, his conception of wartime intelligence is overly circumscribed. What he describes as incapable of performing this crucial task is tactical intelligence. On that point, he is correct. Briggs created the organs of operational intelligence during the Malayan Emergency—the director of intelligence and staff—because tactical intelligence performed a different role. Operational and tactical intelligence are qualitatively different.

A useful model for conceptualizing the role of operational intelligence in organizational learning is John Boyd's observe-orient-decide-act (OODA) loop. Antoine Bousquet noted that the orientation stage distinguishes the OODA formulation from previous cybernetic models.[14] Observation of the environment and opponent—collection activities—provides data for the analysis that orients the system, informs decisions, and implicitly guides subsequent action and observation.[15] When orienting, the system assesses observations using existing analytical frameworks, but also evaluates the utility of those schema to explain its observations by synthesizing what is with what should be.[16] The ability to make sense of a situation and simultaneously refine sense-making mental models imbues the OODA construct with vitality.

The capacity to reorient internally enables an organization to adjust its strategic measures of effectiveness and develop new operational approaches to achieve them. Accomplishing these adjustments through reflection is also the goal of operational design's reframing stage; furthermore, the faculty to do so is an important contribution of operational intelligence. In addition to informing the decisions of commanders, intelligence assesses the outcomes of those decisions and evaluates their effectiveness in accomplishing operational and strategic objectives.[17] Operational intelligence must perpetually evaluate the analytical frameworks that drive decision making.[18] In this way, intelligence makes organizational learning possible.

Because military organizations are hierarchical and commander-centric, organizational learning, aided by operational intelligence, takes place primarily through interaction among the commander and key advisors.[19] Donald Schön concluded that "reflective practitioners" think about the system in which they act through time.[20] Good intelligence places system events in the context of time to aid the commander's understanding.

Vijay Govindarajan and Chris Trimble offered several techniques for reflective practitioners to facilitate strategic innovation and learning, including focusing on critical unknowns instead of concentrating on planning details, considering a plan's underlying assumptions rather than attempting futilely to predict the future, anticipating trends instead of speculating on specifics, conducting frequent historical reviews that produce reminders of past lessons, and measuring leading indicators instead of those that depict present circumstances.[21] These are the questions of understanding and learning. Instead of attempting to predict the future of complex, adaptive systems, these questions seek to illuminate the past in the effort to make sense of the present and anticipate and adapt to the future.[22] These questions look beyond the immediate and tactical, providing a framework for the commander's PIR.

PIRs articulate key questions commanders and planners have about the enemy and the operational environment.[23] They are products of operational decision-making and planning processes and often derive from the decision points identified in the plan.[24] However, as Marc Spinuzzi argued in his paper on commanders' information requirements in complex environments, PIRs must support both execution decisions and adjustment decisions.[25] While the former seek to learn specific future events, the latter drive assessments that indicate a change (or lack of change) in the status quo that may require modifications to the conceptual framework or plan.[26] Thus, operational-level PIRs should ask the questions that help the commander understand the situation and learn from its variations.

The coupling of operational intelligence and operational design reinforces wartime organizational learning. Both aid the intuition and analyses of the organization's central node—the commander. Collective learning also occurs through operational design's intentional use of discourse. Peter Senge argued that optimal organizational learning happens through a systems-thinking approach that involves building a shared vision, recognizing existing mental models, developing teamwork, and encouraging personal mastery of relevant skills.[27] Through discourse, commanders develop and share their understanding of the situation, evaluate competing schema, foster a shared commitment to the organizational goal, and encourage participation in the design of strategies and plans by competent contributors throughout the organization.[28] Operational design's discourse provides the vehicle for collective learning to occur. Operational intelligence elevates the dialogue by introducing rigorous analytical models, intelligence-based descriptions of reality, and the continual cognitive dissonance required to evaluate prevailing conceptual frameworks.

Together, intelligence and design at the operational level of war facilitate organizational learning and innovation. Furthermore, operational design reminds us of operational intelligence's crucial responsibility in accomplishing this function. Over time, intelligence aids the situational understanding of the commander. It provides post-hoc assessments of decisions and evaluates the effectiveness of operations in accomplishing operational and strategic objectives. Furthermore, it reconsiders the utility of existing schema and models for interpreting reality, enabling the organization to reorient or reframe as necessary. The PIRs that shape collection and analysis must reflect the importance of assessments and their contribution to organizational learning. Finally, by participating directly in the discourse, intelligence professionals encourage positive and more rapid learning by the commander and the collective organization.

Collaboration and Operational Intelligence

The collaborative nature of operational design should remind the analyst of the considerable advantage that interaction with commanders, colleagues, and customers yields to the product and process of intelligence. Both intelligence and design benefit enormously from the active participation of the commander. Analysts and designers are, after all, extensions of the commander's mind. When their interaction with the commander is limited, there is a low probability that their processes are responsive to the commander's needs and that their product contributes usefully to the commander's understanding. To the extent design encourages commanders to collaborate, it also benefits operational intelligence.

If commanders are open-minded, collaborative leaders, then directors of intelligence must aggressively pursue opportunities to be collaborative advisors. Much depends on the commander's personality and preferred means of learning. Nevertheless, the intelligence most beneficial to the commander will seldom be found in glossy reports or scripted briefings. Rather, it will be in the active, two-way conversations with chief analysts regarding the nature, tendencies, and relationships of environmental and opposing systems. Templer told his intelligence advisor, Jack Morton, "Mind you, we've got to like each other. It won't work otherwise."[29] Templer was not just being courteous; he expected a very interactive relationship with his intelligence apparatus.

Collaboration should also occur among partners. The role of discourse in operational design is instructive for intelligence not because it is new to the analytical community but because it reminds analysts that there is little room for ego in the endeavor to improve the intelligence product and process. Active engagement by the analyst in a critical dialogue with other knowledgeable analysts raises the understanding of all participants and the likely utility of the scrutinized mental models that explain and anticipate complex situations.

While intelligence classification levels discourage the participation of analysts in a discourse beyond the intelligence community, doing so carries potential benefits. First, analysts share their expertise in a way that elevates the collective understanding of a situation. Second, analysts who frequently interact with their customers are more likely to develop a mutual understanding that can improve the precision of intelligence requirements and tailored products. Third, participation in a semi-open discourse may broaden their customer base to include actors previously unfamiliar with the value of their analytical products.

Under Templer's command, the British army augmented SB with intelligence officers to facilitate reporting from and planning support to tactical forces.[30] These officers provided the connective tissue between SB and front-line units, fostering a dialogue that substantially increased the quality of combat reports made available to SB analysts and the value of intelligence products provided to lower-echelon units. The benefits of collaborative followership, collaborative partnership, and the device of discourse remind intelligence professionals of the teamwork required for success at the operational level of war.

The Joint Intelligence Preparation of the Operational Environment

The most obvious expectation operational design places upon operational intelligence is a systems-thinking approach to understanding the operational environment. Gen James Mattis identified the intelligence director as a "key player in the early design effort" who "leads this effort for the commander."[31] Systems thinking has long been part of intelligence analysis, for which the JIPOE offers a contemporary manifestation.

The JIPOE is both a product and a process. As the former, it embodies a momentary understanding of relevant environmental systems and their interconnections. Capturing this understanding in a report permits its dissemination among key advisors and planners and helps build the collective knowledge of the organization. As a living process, the JIPOE drives intelligence analysts to continually accumulate knowledge on relevant systems and links. As the situation evolves, so must the collective understanding. Therefore, the enhanced knowledge of the analysts who performed the critical thinking required to understand the situation embodies the real product of the JIPOE. Both the report and its creators are crucial to building a shared understanding of the evolving situation.

The Intelligence Designer

Knowledge of the operational design process also reminds the commander of the analyst's central role in the formulation of operational-level approaches. Complex problems are part and parcel of their complex environments, and the two must be understood together. According to designers, as understanding of the situation builds, solutions become self-evident.[32] Who better to aid the commander's conceptualization of the environment and problem than the intelligence analysts who explore and understand the complexities of both? Who better to assess the potential of proposed operational approaches than the intelligence analysts who know the strengths, vulnerabilities, and interrelationships of the environmental and enemy systems subject to action?

There are multiple advantages to including one or more knowledgeable intelligence analysts in the commander's core design team. As implied in the questions above, analysts have the expertise to aid the commander's understanding of a situation. Their expertise also elevates the understanding of other designers and discourse participants. The analyst's depth of understanding provides an intuition that is critical in dynamic situations.[33] The impetus for including intelligence analysts in the core design team is greatest when the corporate understanding of a situation is low and the time available to think is limited. Predictability is not the nature of crisis, and plans are seldom executed as they were developed. When time is compressed, those designers with a deep knowledge of a situation are best positioned to understand quickly the implications of change throughout the relevant systems and assist the commander's reconceptualization of the problem.

Intelligence analysts can help balance the action-prone tendencies of master tacticians, who are commonly found in command and key planning positions. Commanders, designers, and planners inexperienced at the operational level of war are likely to be more comfortable with the capabilities of friendly forces than they are familiar with the complexities of the situation. Knowledge of capabilities is necessary and informs design. However, a fascination with tactical brilliance can also misguide operational approaches.

Millett and Murray, in their analysis of effectiveness during both world wars, noted, "German battlefield superiority only served to encourage appalling strategic myopia. . . . Combat (or tactical) superiority became rationalized as the way to make any strategy work."[34] Paraphrasing historian Russell Weigley, the Germans' tactical and operational reach exceeded their strategic grasp.[35] Similarly, Mahnken cautioned, "Indeed, technical prowess may breed hubris."[36] Coupling the analyst's realism with the tactician's enthusiasm helps balance the discourse and attenuate the siren's call of tactical excellence that can seduce strategic judgment.

Analysts also benefit from their inclusion in the core design team. Frequent interaction with the commander familiarizes the analyst with the commander's concerns and patterns of thinking. Knowledge of the former allows the analyst to better harness operational intelligence activities on behalf of the commander. It may drive adjustments to the collection plan, generate analytical products, and permit the refinement of the commander's PIRs. Meanwhile, a familiarity with the commander's patterns of thought enables the keen analyst to anticipate the commander's concerns and increase the responsiveness of intelligence. Interaction with the commander also familiarizes analysts with the commander's preferred learning techniques so that the analyst can tailor intelligence products to convey information better. Additionally, the commanders' experience and expertise make them among the most insightful analysts in the command. Meaningful dialogue between the commander and the analyst elevates the understanding of both. The analyst's collaboration with other design team members—usually imaginative, critical thinkers themselves—will likewise hone the analyst's thinking. The central placement of the intelligence analyst in the commander's design process benefits all involved.

Not all analysts have what it takes to be a member of the commander's inner circle or core design team. In addition to expertise on a given situation, they must also have rigorous critical thinking skills, the intellectual flexibility to accommodate new ideas and broad perspectives, the creativity to imagine alternate futures, the moral courage to defend unfavorable analysis, and the communication skills to shape the discourse and persuade commanders and fellow designers. Additionally, the analysts must have the necessary rank to participate in a dialogue among rank-conscious actors. Finally, to the extent the commander uses the design team to influence subsequent planning and implementation, the analysts should have direct or indirect authority over the command's collection and analytical activities. In sum, the ideal analyst for the commander's inner circle combines the attributes of the intelligence advisor and the designer.

The Malayan Emergency illustrated the advantage of including the intelligence professional in the commander's core team. Both Briggs and Templer appreciated the role of operational intelligence. They were open-minded men with experience leading and consuming intelligence at the operational level of war. They understood its advantages and limits and chose to elevate its status and responsibility within their commands. Templer expanded and institutionalized the intelligence and organizational reforms that Briggs initiated, including the creation of a director of intelligence. By mid-1952, the function of intelligence achieved a central position in the operational-level command's organization and processes, as symbolized by the membership of Morton, director of intelligence, on the operations committee. To the extent there was a core design team in Malaya, the operations committee was it. While intelligence alone did not win the Malayan Emergency, there is an unmistakable positive correlation between the effectiveness of the counterinsurgency and the effectiveness of intelligence. The inclusion of the key intelligence advisor in the commander's core design team was an innovative part of the success.

Conclusions

Operational intelligence and operational design are symbiotic partners that enrich operational art. They are complex cognitive processes intended to assist the commander's understanding of the situation. They share a responsibility to enable effective, dynamic, uncertainty-tolerant operations on behalf of the commander. While the operational design literature includes little that is new or unfamiliar to the intelligence community, the operational design process provides several key reminders to intelligence professionals at the operational level of war.

First, the tension between serving the commander and facilitating tactical action must favor the commander. Operational intelligence is not simply tactical reconnaissance writ large. While it identifies opportunities and vulnerabilities for exploitation, it also informs the design of the operational approach. Operational intelligence best supports individual Soldiers, Sailors, Airmen, and Marines by helping the commander conceptualize winning operational concepts that lead to desired strategic outcomes.

Second, operational intelligence provides the command the vital capacity to learn and innovate by continually assessing the consequences of decisions and operations as they relate to the accomplishment of strategic and operational goals. Furthermore, by evaluating the utility of the conceptual frameworks that guide decisions and action, intelligence professionals enable their commands to reframe evolving situations and reorient operations.

Third, for operational intelligence to achieve its full potential, intelligence professionals must regularly and openly collaborate with the commander, other analysts, and customers throughout the command. Cultivating a collaborative relationship with the commander is most significant for the success of operational intelligence. Open, engaging, and frequent dialogue pays dividends to all involved.

Fourth, designers and planners rely on the systems analyses conducted by intelligence professionals and captured in the JIPOE. Strategists, analysts, and planners must use the JIPOE to elevate their own understanding of the situation's complexity. However, the most important JIPOE products are the analysts who developed situational awareness through their critical thinking about the environmental and opposing systems. Wherever possible, these key human resources should provide the leaven to design and planning teams.

Finally, expert analysts belong foremost in positions that are central to the commander's conceptualization of the environment, problem, and operational approach—the core design team. Their inclusion benefits the commander, the design process, and the analyst's ability to harness operational intelligence on behalf of the commander. Not every expert analyst will be a good fit for the responsibility of joining the commander's inner circle. However, the ideal advisor will embody the virtues of analytical expertise, intellectual flexibility, imagination, moral courage, and strong communication skills.

That advisor—the intelligence designer—will address strategic matters without ignoring tactical ones; facilitate learning by an organization, especially by its commander; build a collaborative relationship with the commander and key staff; convey a systems understanding of the environment and opponent; and help design the effective operational approaches that achieve the appropriate operational objectives that solve wicked problems. He or she will synthesize the complementary activities of operational intelligence and operational design. In sum, the intelligence designer will offer the flexible-minded and collaborative commander foreknowledge through understanding the enemy situation, operational environment, strategic goals, and tactical realities.

Notes

1. Lindley, *Understanding Uncertainty*, xi.

2. Sun Tzu, *Illustrated Art of War*, 232.

3. Gray, *Explorations in Strategy*, 61; also see notes in chapter 2. Colin Gray defined tactics and strategy as such: "Namely, whereas tactics is the realm of the actual employment of armed forces, strategy refers to the intended or real consequences of the use of forces for the course and outcome of a war."

4. Almost by definition, the operational approach will likely have prominent military features. However, the predominance of military activities within an operational approach will vary depending on the kind of war—regular or irregular—and various circumstances. Depending on those circumstances, it is also possible that the operational approach can do no better than address the symptoms of the underlying problem in the hope that doing so will facilitate the execution of other elements of strategy that can address the problem but are outside the purview of the operational commander.

5. Bracketed words are those of the original authors. See Millett and Murray, "Introduction," xvi.

6. Cushman, "Challenge and Response," 322, 335.

7. Mahnken, *Technology and the American Way*, 6.

8. US Air Forces Central's airpower summaries.

9. Hebert, "Compressing the Kill Chain," 50–54.

10. Rosen, *Winning the Next War*, 29–39.

11. Ibid., 35. Rosen defined a strategic measure of effectiveness as "taken together, the definition of the strategic goal, the relationship of military operations to that goal, and indicators of how well operations are proceeding."

12. Ibid.

13. Ibid., 30.

14. Bousquet, *Scientific Way of Warfare*, 188.

15. Ibid.

16. Ibid., 189.

17. Handel, *Leadership and Intelligence*, 9; JP 2-0, *Joint Intelligence*, I-8, IV-6; and chapter 3 of this paper.

18. Bousquet, *Scientific Way of Warfare*, 190. Bousquet describes Boyd's process of analytical "destruction and creation." I assert that this is (or should be) a contribution of operational intelligence.

19. Rosen, *Winning the Next War*, 38–39. Rosen argues that when innovation occurs in hierarchical and centralized organizations, it is more likely to be more far-reaching and rapid.

20. Schön, *Reflective Practitioner*, 291.

21. Govindarajan and Trimble, "Strategic Innovation," 70–74; and chapter 6 of this paper.

22. Govindarajan and Trimble, "Strategic Innovation," 74.

23. JP 2-0, *Joint Intelligence*, I-8; and chapter 3 of this paper.

24. JP 2-01, *Joint and National Intelligence*, II-2; and Spinuzzi, "CCIR for Complex," 18–22.

25. Spinuzzi, "CCIR for Complex," 18.

26. Ibid., 97.

27. Senge, *Fifth Discipline*, 12.

28. See chapter 7 of this paper.

29. Cloake, *Templer*, 229; and chapter 5 of this paper.

30. Sunderland, "Antiguerrilla Intelligence in Malaya," 27; and chapter 5 of this paper.

31. Mattis, "Vision for a Joint Approach."

32. Schmitt, "A Systemic Concept"; and chapter 7 of this paper.

33. For more on the role of expertise in building intuition and the role of intuition in decision making in dynamic situations, see Klein, *Power of Intuition*, and Gladwell, *Blink*. A useful argument for critical thinking and against reliance on intuition is made in LeGault, *Think!* My point is that when there is limited time to think, the expert's intuition is more useful than that of the amateur.

34. Murray and Millett, "Introduction," xiii.

35. Weigley, "Political and Strategic Dimensions," 363.

36. Mahnken, *American Way of War*, 6.

Chapter 10

Conclusions

If we should have to fight, we should be prepared to do so from
the neck up instead of from the neck down.

—Jimmy Doolittle

Uncertainty is an inescapable part of war, and thinking is too often an undervalued activity within it. "Wicked" problems and the complex, adaptive systems that produce them generate uncertainty; the imperative for action in war decreases patience for the critical analysis required to solve complex problems. Both operational intelligence and operational design endeavor to mitigate uncertainty in war and aim to guide conflict thoughtfully toward the accomplishment of operational and strategic objectives, bridging tactical action to strategic outcome.

The intelligence analyst and the operational designer are extensions of the commander's mind. The analyst seeks to ask and answer the right questions; the designer strives to identify and solve the right problems. Analysts collect and analyze information to build understanding of a complex operational situation; designers translate understanding into an approach for achieving operational aims and strategic ends. Analysts endeavor to make sense of historical and current circumstances to inform future action; designers labor to shape the future based on what is learned from the past and known about the present. Without uncertainty in war, there would be no need for operational intelligence or operational design; because of uncertainty in war, operational intelligence and operational design are harnessed to the same yoke.

This project evaluated how emerging concepts of operational design should influence the practice of intelligence at the operational level of war. It began with an analysis of operational intelligence, including a historical assessment of its role in the 1948–60 Malayan Emergency. It then considered operational design, including a design-based reassessment of the Malayan Emergency. Finally, it synthesized insights from both operational intelligence and operational design to produce lessons for commanders and intelligence professionals. This conclusion summarizes the project's major findings and considers some implications for the organization, training, and equipment required for effective operational intelligence in the information age.

Operational Intelligence

Operational intelligence is state activity to understand foreign entities and potential battlespaces for planning and conducting campaigns and major operations; perforce, it must include some consideration of strategy and tactics. It is, fundamentally, intelligence at the operational level of war, and it informs the alignment of tactical employment with strategic objectives.

The practice of operational intelligence involves the collection of information about the adversary and the battlespace and the analysis of that data to produce knowledge and insight. Data are collected from a variety of secret and overt sources. Directors of intelligence must balance their support to subordinate forces, planners, and commanders. While assistance to lower-echelon forces facilitates action, the operational-level commander serves strategy and owns operations and campaigns.[1] Successful analysis requires critical thinking, including an awareness of cognitive biases and the limitations of intelligence. Systems analyses, such as that recorded in the JIPOE, help build a realistic understanding of the adversary and the battlespace, which supports plan development and the operational-level commander's decision-making process. Ultimately, intelligence outputs—advice, estimates, and assessments—must support the commander. Operational intelligence professionals are, after all, an extension of the commander's mind.

Operational intelligence is not a substitute for the commander's judgment; rather, it aids it. Commanders must understand how to exploit intelligence effectively. The attributes of the commander and the intelligence advisor and the partnership between them are crucial to the successful use of operational intelligence. The ideal relationship is open and engaging with frequent and regular interaction. It is mutually respectful without becoming personal. The commander ensures that the intelligence advisor is an integral part of his or her inner circle but also permits the advisor the degree of autonomy necessary for objective analysis. The ideal advisor is an exemplar of critical analytical and communication skills, intellectual flexibility, and courage. The traits of the commander are most critical to the optimal use of operational intelligence. Personality, experience leading intelligence, and self-perceptions of vulnerability and expertise shape the commander's use of intelligence. Open-minded commanders tolerate uncertainty and alternative viewpoints. Experienced commanders are familiar with the capabilities and limits of intelligence. Aggressive and risk-tolerant commanders are most sensitive to the opportunities and dangers revealed by their intelligence. Commanders who exemplify open-mindedness, are experienced, and have a preference for aggressive operational concepts are best suited to exploit operational intelligence in their decision making.

Operational Intelligence
in the Malayan Emergency

The Malayan Emergency is an intelligence success story, though intelligence alone did not win the counterinsurgency. Intelligence—along with psychological operations, population control, dynamic leadership, organizational learning, and policies of decolonization and Malayanization—contributed to the emergency's successful conclusion. Nevertheless, the positive correlation between effective intelligence and effective counterinsurgency is impressive. Operational intelligence and operational effectiveness maintained a multifarious, reinforcing relationship that produced steadily increasing mutual gains. As intelligence improved, security did as well. As security improved, Chinese civilians provided the information needed to defeat the insurgency.

At the emergency's start, intelligence and security operations were in disarray. British intelligence failed to recognize or take seriously the emergence of a communist insurgency during the late 1940s. An ill-advised counterterrorism strategy that delayed counterinsurgency progress by as much as two years came from an insufficient understanding of the problem.

The intelligence system in Malaya was still in generally poor condition when Lt Gen Sir Harold Briggs arrived in 1950. Briggs appeared to derive his prescient conceptualization of the operational environment and problem from an amalgam of sources, including improving intelligence assessments. He placed enormous importance on intelligence and improved the system to the extent permitted by his limited authority, including the advent of the director of intelligence position to shoulder the responsibilities that lay beyond tactical intelligence. Briggs's most important contribution to the emergency's eventual success was creating the Briggs Plan that set the conditions for victory.

Gen Sir Gerald Templer's energetic execution of the Briggs Plan produced substantial counterinsurgency gains. Furthermore, his progressive intelligence reforms invigorated both intelligence and operations. He removed bureaucratic barriers to effective collection and analysis and improved operations by making intelligence integral to planning and execution. Templer's experience with and appreciation of intelligence prepared him to lead his intelligence apparatus. He did so in partnership with an empowered and capable intelligence director with whom he enjoyed a special relationship crucial to the successful exploitation of operational intelligence.

Operational Design

Operational design uses design concepts to address the complex problems facing commanders at the operational level of war. It represents an application of systems theory to operational art. Systems thinking enables an appreciation of complex, adaptive systems and their continual change. It also assists designers in identifying and solving the ill-structured, wicked problems found in social systems. Designers grapple with social challenges through a mental process by which they conceptualize the problem as a product of its environment, invent a solution, visualize the problem-solution relationship, appraise the solution, and learn through reflection.

Design helps mitigate complexity. Its systems-thinking approach stimulates a holistic appreciation of the problem and solution, thereby partly closing the gap between understanding and reality. Its collaborative elements allow for the plural decision making often necessary in social systems. Additionally, its iterative nature gives it the flexibility to accommodate the uncertainty and dynamism inherent in complex problems. Design is well suited to address complex social challenges, including those found in war.

Operational design applies the tools of design to the complex problems of war. Carl von Clausewitz admonished that determining the kind of war that is to be undertaken is the most essential of all judgments made by the statesman and commander. Operational design assists this consequential assessment at the operational level.

Operational design occurs in addition to planning. It enriches operational art through systems thinking, collaborative leadership, iterative decision making, and organizational learning. Additionally, it places special emphasis on distilling a problem down to its root causes. Operational design entails concurrent, supportive endeavors to understand the interconnected operational environment in which the problem exists and potential action will occur; the problem itself, in all its complexity; and the most effective approach to solve the problem. The operational approach emerges from a growing appreciation of the situation.

Operational design is a commander-led process that employs an inclusive and critical discourse to analyze concepts, synthesize ideas, cultivate learning, and promote a shared understanding of the problem that drives the organization toward an effective operational approach. Design teams represent an extension of the commander's mind whose purpose is not to think on behalf of the commander but to assist the commander's critical and creative conceptualization of looming complex challenges.

Operational Design
in the Malayan Emergency

The Malayan Emergency is an instructive historical example that highlights certain elements of operational design. Collaborative leadership and discourse were crucial to the development of understanding for both Briggs and Templer. Briggs's appreciation of the complex operational environment and wicked problem that was the emergency prompted him to reframe the challenge as one of good governance. He concluded that the current counterterrorism strategy was inadequate because it could not address the root problem of Chinese disenfranchisement. The winning Briggs Plan emerged from his improved understanding.

Templer developed his own appreciation of the situation upon arriving in Malaya and determined that reframing was unnecessary. His understanding of the operational environment, the problem, and the optimal operational approach mirrored that of Briggs. He implemented the Briggs Plan with verve and dynamism. Furthermore, he surrounded himself with a core design team comprised of key stakeholders within his command, including his director of intelligence.

Synthesis of Operational Intelligence
and Operational Design

Operational intelligence and operational design are symbiotic cognitive processes that enrich operational art. They both assist the commander's understanding of the operational situation and share a duty to enable effective, dynamic, uncertainty-tolerant operations. While little in the operational design literature is novel to the intelligence community, the operational design process provides several significant reminders to intelligence professionals at the operational level of war.

First, the balance between serving the commander and supporting tactical action must tilt toward the commander. Operational intelligence is not tactical reconnaissance writ large. It best assists lower-echelon forces by aiding the commander's design of a winning operational approach that achieves desired strategic outcomes.

Second, operational intelligence enables organizational learning in the command by continually assessing the consequences of decisions and operations as they relate to the accomplishment of strategic and operational goals. Additionally, by evaluating the utility of the conceptual frameworks that guide decisions and action, intelligence professionals enable their commanders, hence their organizations, to reframe changing situations and reorient operations.

Third, to achieve the full potential of operational intelligence, intelligence professionals must collaborate with the commander, other analysts, and customers throughout the command. The cultivation of a collaborative relationship with the commander is most significant for the success of operational intelligence. An open, engaging, frequent, two-way dialogue pays dividends to all involved.

Fourth, designers and planners rely on the systems analyses conducted by intelligence professionals and captured in the JIPOE. Strategists, analysts, and planners use the JIPOE to elevate their own understanding of the situation's complexity. However, the most important products of the JIPOE process are the analysts themselves. They developed situational awareness through their critical thinking about the environmental and opposing systems, becoming invaluable commodities in the organization. Wherever possible, these key human resources should matrix across the command to provide design and planning teams the leaven of operational intelligence.

Finally, expert analysts belong foremost as central fixtures in the commander's inner circle and core design team where they can best assist the commander's conceptualization of the environment, problem, and operational approach. Their inclusion benefits the commander, the design process, and the analyst's ability to harness the strength of operational intelligence. Not every expert analyst will be suited for the responsibility of performing in the commander's inner circle. The ideal advisor will embody the virtues of analytical expertise, intellectual flexibility, imagination, moral courage, and strong communication skills.

That advisor—the intelligence-designer—will be the analyst who can address strategic matters and tactical ones; encourage organizational learning, especially through that of the commander; cultivate a collaborative relationship with the commander and key staff; impart a systems understanding of the environment and opponent; and help construct effective operational approaches that achieve the operational objectives that solve wicked problems. He or she will synthesize the complementary activities of operational intelligence and operational design to offer the flexible-minded and collaborative commander an otherwise unavailable level of foreknowledge.

Implications

From the synthesis of operational intelligence and operational design emerges a deeper understanding of both processes, which also reveals several implications for the education, training, and equipping of the joint force. Because operational intelligence informs the alignment of tactical action with strategic objectives, commanders must balance two inherent, related tensions: one—between tactics and strategy—is part of operational art, and the other—between collection and analysis—is endemic to intelligence. Disequilibrium in either decreases the effectiveness of operational intelligence ergo joint operations and elevates the risk of intelligence failure at the operational level of war. Alarmingly, current trends suggest that the balances tilt toward collection in support of tactical operations.

Intelligence failure is a tired accusation that often more accurately reveals the speaker's ignorance of intelligence than it describes the underlying reasons for a particular surprise. Failures occur when an existing capability to collect preventive information is not employed or when such information is collected but not understood. As Richard Betts explained, when surprises happen—which is inevitable in our complex world—they are seldom the fault of collectors. Sometimes the surprises are the oversight of the analysts and, most commonly, the negligence of the decision makers whose policies, plans, and questions drive the intelligence process.[2] At the operational level of war, commanders make the decisions. Therefore, in general, an intelligence failure is a failure of command.

To succeed, operational-level commanders must balance the tension between tactics and strategy, both essential to effective operations. Tactics without strategy lack purpose, and strategy without tactics is toothless. Nevertheless, as Allan R. Millett and Williamson Murray argued in their landmark work *Military Effectiveness*, no amount of tactical virtuosity can compensate for errors in strategic judgment. Tactical mistakes may be costly, but strategic ones "live forever."[3]

In today's fight, operational intelligence professionals and organizations concentrate on the employment of ISR assets—traditional and otherwise—to facilitate tactical action. The overwatch of friendly ground forces and the sensor-shooter couplings in modern airpower's "kill chain" represent two examples of how ISR contributes to the execution of combat power. Commanders are correct to enable tactical action by augmenting the force-multiplying ISR capabilities organic to lower-echelon forces. While intelligence support to tactics should seldom come at the expense of the operation or campaign, refusing to assist tactical units is almost never a palatable choice.

To succeed, commanders must also balance the tension between collection and analysis. The recent investment in and proliferation of sensors and platforms enhance collection, and increasingly powerful ISR capabilities discern very small objects and momentary events. However, collection alone does not produce intelligence. Analysis is "the thinking part of the intelligence process," according to James Bruce and Roger George.[4] The questions of tactical intelligence are numerous in war, but typically demand little analytical depth. Making sense of the complex problems that challenge the operational commander requires a significant and perpetual analytical investment. Together, operational-level collection and analysis assist commanders with conceptualizing the operational environment, its problems, and winning operational approaches. In this way, balanced ISR reduces the chances of surprise and increases the probability that tactical action achieves strategic objectives. Nevertheless, refusing to assist tactical units with the support they require is not a viable alternative.

Recent joint force ISR enhancements and experiences employing ISR capabilities threaten to institutionalize an imbalanced understanding of operational intelligence that favors collection and tactical intelligence. Maintaining the proper balance within operational intelligence is possible only through the strengthening of the joint force's analytical capacity. Provided are four long-term suggestions to refocus operational intelligence:

1. The most promising way to ensure the long-term equilibrium of operational intelligence is through the education of future commanders, intelligence advisors, and staffs. Most professional officers are more comfortable with tactics than with operational-level concepts, and their understanding of intelligence is skewed similarly. The schools of professional military education are responsible for preparing future commanders and their advisors for the peculiar demands of operational-level leadership. The schools' curricula must prominently feature the proper role, purposes, priorities, strengths, and limits of operational intelligence in the design and prosecution of operations and campaigns.

2. Joint force processes and systems must better aggregate collected information—regardless of its source, location, or classification—for central, operational-level analysis. While the questions of tactical- and operational-level analysis differ, tactical units and sensors can collect data relevant to operational-level analysis. Development of the systems and training required to push that information into central databases in intelligible, reference-friendly formats would increase the efficiency

of operational intelligence and decrease, in part, the struggle for limited ISR assets.

3. The joint community can create incentives for the development and retention of operational-level analysts—including intelligence designers—by establishing rigorous education, training, and experience requirements for key joint intelligence positions at the field-grade, colonel, and general officer levels. This would encourage the services to invest in and value officers with the skills and experiences needed to advance in the joint intelligence community. In turn, through the development and retention of such officers, the services would propagate a balanced understanding of operational intelligence that would best enable the joint force and its commanders to think through uncertainty at the operational level of war.

4. Equipping both operational-level headquarters units and tactical-level units with sufficient, dedicated ISR collection and analytical capabilities to satisfy their wartime intelligence requirements would alleviate much of the tension within operational intelligence. While perhaps not resource efficient, this recommendation would do more than signal tacitly the importance of intelligence to operations; it would equip the joint force to perform intelligence-led campaigns and operations.

From the study of operational design emerges a deeper understanding of the role required of operational intelligence. Operational intelligence is not simply tactical reconnaissance writ large. It informs the alignment of tactics and strategy through its facilitation of a shared systems understanding of the operational environment and problem by the commander and key staff. An operational approach materializes from this understanding that seeks to address the underlying causes of the operational, or strategic, problem. Operational intelligence also enables organizational learning by evaluating the effectiveness of operational approaches and the cognitive schema used to create them. Services must develop and retain analysts with superior expertise, mental flexibility, imagination, courage, and communication skills who will aid operational-level commanders in thinking through their challenges. These analysts belong in central positions alongside the commander and in core design and planning teams. Additionally, such intelligence professionals should focus the collection and analysis of operational-level and tactical-level ISR to enable effective operations and campaigns. When employed by an open-minded and collaborative commander, the complementary processes of operational intelligence and operational design will enrich operational art in the information age.

Notes

1. The operational-level commander is from the top-down perspective a servant of strategy; however, the commander's advice and the outcomes of the operations and campaigns will also shape strategy.

2. Betts, "Analysis, War, and Decision," 61.

3. Murray and Millett , "Introduction," xvi.

4. Bruce and George, "Intelligence Analysis," 1.

Abbreviations

CAS	complex adaptive system
CEP/SEP	captured and surrendered enemy personnel
CIA	Central Intelligence Agency
DIOCC	Defense Intelligence Operations Coordination Center
DMI	director of military intelligence
EBO	effects-based operations
EO	executive order
FM	field manual
I&W	indications and warning
IADS	integrated air and missile defense system
IDF	Israeli Defense Forces
ISR	intelligence, surveillance, and reconnaissance
J-2	joint staff
JIPOE	joint intelligence preparation of the operational environment
JP	joint publication
JWFC	Joint Warfighting Center
MCP	Malayan Communist Party
MSS	Malayan Security Service
OODA	observe-orient-decide-act
OTRI	Operational Theory Research Institute
PIR	priority intelligence requirement
SB	Special Branch
SOD	systemic operational design
TRADOC	Training and Doctrine Command

Bibliography

Abb, Madelfia A. "A Living Military System on the Verge of Annihilation." Unpublished monograph. Ft. Leavenworth, KS: School of Advanced Military Studies, 10 May 2000.

Air Force Doctrine Document 2-9. *Intelligence, Surveillance, and Reconnaissance Operations*, 17 July 2007.

Air Force Tactics, Techniques, and Procedures 3-3.AOC. *Operational Employment–Air and Space Operations Center*, 1 November 2007.

"Airpower Summaries." US Air Forces Central. Accessed 12 May 2011. http://www.afcent.af.mil/news/pressreleases/index.asp.

Allen, Robert S. *Lucky Forward*. New York: Vanguard Press, 1947.

Andrew, Christopher. "American Presidents and Their Intelligence Communities." In *Analyzing Intelligence: Origins, Obstacles, and Innovations*, edited by Roger Z. George and James B. Bruce, 431–45. Washington, DC: Georgetown University Press, 2008.

———. "Churchill and Intelligence." In *Leaders and Intelligence*, edited by Michael I. Handel, 181–93. Totowa, NJ: Frank Cass, 1989.

Arnett, Eric H. "Welcome to Hyperwar." *The Bulletin of the Atomic Scientists* 48, no. 7 (September 1992): 14–21.

Arquilla, John, and David Ronfeldt. "Cyberwar Is Coming!" *Comparative Strategy* 12, no. 2 (Spring 1993): 152–55.

Austin, N. J. E., and N. B. Rankov. *Exploratio: Military and Political Intelligence in the Roman World from the Second Punic War to the Battle of Adrianople*. New York: Routledge, 1995.

Ayer, Fred, Jr. *Before the Colors Fade*. Boston: Houghton Mifflin, 1964.

Barabasi, Albert-Laszlo. *Linked: The New Science of Networks*. Cambridge, MA: Perseus Publishing, 2002.

Barber, James David. *The Presidential Character: Predicting Performance in the White House*. 4th ed. Englewood Cliffs, NJ: Prentice-Hall, 1985.

Barber, Noel. *The War of the Running Dogs: The Malayan Emergency: 1948–1960*. New York: Weybright and Talley, 1971.

Bar-Joseph, Uri. "Intelligence Failure and the Need for Cognitive Closure: The Case of Yom Kippur." In *Paradoxes of Strategic Intelligence: Essays in Honour of Michael I. Handel*, edited by Richard Betts and Thomas Mahnken. London: Frank Cass, 2003.

Bennett, Huw. " 'A Very Salutary Effect': The Counter-Terror Strategy in the Early Malayan Emergency, June 1948 to December 1949." *Journal of Strategic Studies* 32, no. 3 (June 2009): 415–44.

Berkowitz, Bruce D., and Allan E. Goodman. *Best Truth: Intelligence in the Information Age*. New Haven, CT: Yale University Press, 2000.

Bertalanffy, Ludwig von. "The Theory of Open Systems in Physics and Biology." *Science* 111, no. 2872 (January 1950): 23–29.

Betts, Richard K. "Analysis, War, and Decision: Why Intelligence Failures Are Inevitable." *World Politics* 31, no. 1 (October 1978): 61–89.

———. *Enemies of Intelligence: Knowledge & Power in American National Security*. New York: Columbia University Press, 2007.

———. "The New Politics of Intelligence: Will Reforms Work This Time?" *Foreign Affairs* 83, no. 3 (May/June 2004): 2–8.

———. "Surprise, Scholasticism, and Strategy: A Review of Ariel Levite's Intelligence and Strategic Surprises." *International Studies Quarterly* 33, no. 3 (September 1989): 329–43.

Beyerchen, Alan. "Clausewitz, Nonlinearity, and the Unpredictability of War." *International Security* 17, no. 3 (Winter 1992–93): 59–90.

Blakesley, Lance. *Presidential Leadership: From Eisenhower to Clinton*. Chicago: Nelson-Hall Publishers, 1995.

Blakesley, Paul J. "Operational Shock and Complexity Theory." Unpublished monograph. Ft. Leavenworth, KS: School of Advanced Military Studies, 26 May 2005.

Boulding, Kenneth E. "General Systems Theory—The Skeleton of Science." *Management Science* 2, no. 3 (April 1956): 134.

Bousquet, Antoine. *The Scientific Way of Warfare: Order and Chaos on the Battlefields of Modernity*. New York: Columbia University Press, 2009.

Boyd, John. "Patterns of Conflict." Edited by Chet Richards and Chuck Spinney. Washington, DC: Defense and the National Interest, 1995.

Brate, Adam. *Technomanifestos: Visions from the Information Revolutionaries*. New York: Texere, 2002.

Brauner, Marygail K., Hugh G. Massey, S. Craig Moore, and Darren D. Medlin. *Improving Development and Utilization of U.S. Air Force Intelligence Officers*. Santa Monica, CA: RAND Corporation, 2009.

Bruce, James B. "Making Analysis More Reliable: Why Epistemology Matters to Intelligence." In *Analyzing Intelligence: Origins, Obstacles, and Innovations*, edited by Roger Z. George and James B. Bruce, 171–90. Washington, DC: Georgetown University Press, 2008.

———. "The Missing Link: The Analyst-Collector Relationship." In *Analyzing Intelligence: Origins, Obstacles, and Innovations*, edited by Roger Z. George and James B. Bruce, 191–210. Washington DC: Georgetown University Press, 2008.

Bruce, James B., and Roger Z. George. "Intelligence Analysis—The Emergence of a Discipline." In *Analyzing Intelligence: Origins, Obstacles, and Innovations*, edited by Roger Z George and James B. Bruce, 1–15. Washington, DC: Georgetown University Press, 2008.

Brugioni, Dino A. *Eyes in the Sky: Eisenhower, the CIA, and Cold War Aerial Espionage*. Washington, DC: Naval Institute Press, 2010.

Buchanan, Bruce. *The Citizen's Presidency: Standards of Choice and Judgment*. Washington, DC: Congressional Quarterly, 1987.

Bundy, William P. "The Guiding of Intelligence Collection." *Studies in Intelligence* 3, no. 1 (Winter 1959): 37–53.

Burgess, Ronald L. "Operational Intelligence: Is It a Panacea?" Unpublished monograph. Ft. Leavenworth, KS: School of Advanced Military Studies, 21 April 1987.

Caesar, Julius. *Caesar's Commentaries: On the Gallic War & On The Civil War*. Edited by James H. Ford. Translated by W. A. MacDevitt. El Paso, TX: El Paso Norte Press, 2005.

Campbell, David P. "The Psychological Test Profiles of Brigadier Generals: Warmongers or Decisive Warriors?" In *Assessing Individual Differences in Human Behavior: New Concepts, Methods, and Findings*, edited by David J. Lubinski and Renee V. Dawis, 145–75. Palo Alto, CA: Davies-Black Publishing, 1995.

Central Intelligence Agency. Executive Order 12333. Accessed 21 March 2011. https://www.cia.gov/about-cia/eo12333.html.

Chan, Steve. "The Intelligence of Stupidity: Understanding Failures in Strategic Warning." *The American Political Science Review* 73, no. 1 (March 1979): 171–80.

Checkland, Peter. *Systems Thinking, Systems Practice*. New York: John Wiley & Sons, 1993.

Clausewitz, Carl von. *On War*. Edited by Michael Howard and Peter Paret. Princeton, NJ: Princeton University Press, 1976.

Cloake, John. *Templer: Tiger of Malaya*. London: Harrap Limited, 1985.

Clutterbuck, Richard L. *The Long Long War: Counterinsurgency in Malaya and Vietnam*. New York: Praeger, 1966.

Coates, John. *Suppressing Insurgency: An Analysis of the Malayan Emergency, 1948–1954*. Boulder, CO: Westview Press, 1992.

Conklin, Jeff. *Dialogue Mapping: Building Shared Understanding of Wicked Problems*. Chichester, England: John Wiley & Sons, Ltd., 2006.

Cranz, Donald. "Understanding Change: Sigismund von Schlichting and the Operational Level of War." Unpublished monograph. Ft. Leavenworth, KS: School of Advanced Military Studies, 1989.

Cross, Nigel. "The Nature and Nurture of the Design Ability." *Design Studies* 11, no. 3 (1990): 127–40.

Cushman, John H. "Challenge and Response at the Operational and Tactical Levels, 1914–45." In *Military Effectiveness*, edited by Allan R. Millett and Williamson Murray. Vol. 3, *The Second World* War, 320–40. New York: Cambridge University Press, 2010.

Davison, Ketti G. "Systemic Operational Design (SOD): Gaining and Maintaining the Cognitive Initiative." Unpublished monograph. Ft. Leavenworth, KS: School of Advanced Military Studies, 25 May 2006.

De Grimoard, Philippe Henri. "Treatise on Service in the Army General Staff: Reflections on its Organization and Functions, in Administrative and Military Respect." Edited by Rick Sanders. *Studies in Intelligence* 54, no. 2 (June 2010): 37–40.

Deptula, David A. *Effects-Based Operations: Change in the Nature of Warfare.* Defense and Airpower Series, Arlington, VA: Aerospace Education Foundation, 2001.

———. "Think Different." *Armed Forces Journal* 148, no. 4 (November 2010): 20–39.

Deptula, David, and Greg Brown. "A House Divided: The Indivisibility of Intelligence, Surveillance, and Reconnaissance." *Air & Space Power Journal* 22, no. 2 (Summer 2005): 5–15.

Deutsch, Harold C. "Commanding Generals and the Uses of Intelligence." In *Leaders and Intelligence*, edited by Michael I. Handel, 194–260. Totowa, NJ: Frank Cass, 1989.

Dickson, Keith D. *Operational Design: A Methodology for Planners.* Norfolk, VA: Joint and Combined Warfighting School, Spring 2007.

DiPasquale, Joseph A. "Discourse in Systemic Operational Design." Unpublished monograph. Ft. Leavenworth, KS: School of Advanced Military Studies, 22 May 2007.

Drea, Edward J. *MacArthur's ULTRA: Codebreaking and the War against Japan.* Lawrence, KS: University Press of Kansas, 1991.

Dulles, Allen. *The Craft of Intelligence: America's Legendary Spy Master on the Fundamentals of Intelligence Gathering for a Free World.* Guilford, CT: The Lyons Press, 2006.

Dyson, Freeman. "A Failure of Intelligence: Operational Research at RAF Bomber Command, 1943–1945." *Technology Review* 109, no. 5 (November/December 2006): 62–71.

Eisenhower, John S. D. *The Bitter Woods: The Battle of the Bulge.* New York: Da Capo Press, Inc., 1995.

Elder, Gregory. "Intelligence in War: It Can Be Decisive." *Studies in Intelligence* 50, no. 2 (2006): 13–25.

Elder, Linda, and Richard Paul. *The Foundations of Analytic Thinking: How to Take Thinking Apart and What to Look for When You Do*. Dillon Bay, CA: The Foundation for Critical Thinking, 2003.

Elkus, Adam, and Crispin Burke. "Operational Design: Promise and Problems." *smallwarsjournal.com*. Accessed 10 December 2010. http://small warsjournal.com/blog/journal/docs-temp/362-elkus.pdf.

Fadok, David S. "John Boyd and John Warden: Air Power's Quest for Strategic Paralysis." Unpublished thesis, Maxwell AFB, AL: School of Advanced Airpower Studies, February 1995.

Field Manual 2-0, *Intelligence*, March 2010.

Field Manual 3-0, *Operations*, February 2009.

Field Manual 5-0, *The Operations Process*, March 2010.

Flynn, Michael T., Matt Pottinger, and Paul D. Batchelor. *Fixing Intel: A Blueprint for Making Intelligence Relevant in Afghanistan*. Washington, DC: Center for a New American Security, January 2010.

Friedman, Thomas L. *The World Is Flat: A Brief History of the 21st Century*. New York: Farrar, Straus and Giroux, 2006.

Gates, Robert M. "Guarding against Politicization." *Studies in Intelligence* 36, no. 1 (1992): 5–13.

Gazit, Shlomo. "Estimates and Fortune-Telling in Intelligence Work." *International Security* 4, no. 4 (Spring 1980): 36–56.

———. "Intelligence Estimates and the Decision-Maker." In *Leaders and Intelligence*, edited by Michael I. Handel, 261–87. Totowa, NJ: Frank Cass, 1989.

George, Alexander L., and Juliette L. George. *Presidential Personality and Performance*. Boulder, CO: Westview Press, 1998.

Gieryn, T. F. *Science and Social Structure: A Festschrift for Robert K. Merton*. New York: New York Academy of Sciences, 1980.

Gladwell, Malcolm. *Blink: The Power of Thinking without Thinking*. New York: Back Bay Books, 2005.

———. *The Tipping Point: How Little Things Can Make a Big Difference*. New York: Little, Brown and Company, 2002.

Goerlitz, Walter. *History of the German General Staff, 1657–1945*. Westport, CT: Greenwood Press, 1975.

Govindarajan, Vijay, and Chris Trimble. "Strategic Innovation and the Science of Learning." *MIT Sloan Management Review* 45, no. 2 (Winter 2004): 66–75.

Gray, Colin S. *Explorations in Strategy*. Westport, CT: Praeger Publishers, 1998.

———. "Stability Operations in Strategic Perspective: A Skeptical View." *Parameters* 36, no. 2 (Summer 2006): 4–14.

Guevara, Ernesto. *Guerrilla Warfare*. New York: Praeger, 1961.

Gutjahr, Melanie M. H. *The Intelligence Archipelago: The Community's Struggle to Reform in a Globalized Era*. Washington, DC: Center for Strategic Intelligence Research, 2005.

Hack, Karl. "British Intelligence and Counter-Insurgency in the Era of Decolonisation: The Example of Malaya." *Intelligence and National Security* 14, no. 2 (Summer 1999): 124–55.

———. "Corpses, Prisoners of War and Captured Documents: British and Communist Narratives of the Malayan Emergency, and the Dynamics of Intelligence Transformation." *Intelligence and National Security* 14, no. 4 (Winter 1999): 211–41.

———. "The Malayan Emergency as Counter-Insurgency Paradigm." *Journal of Strategic Studies* 32, no. 3 (June 2009): 383–414.

Haggerty, K. D., and R. V. Ericson. "The Surveillant Assemblage." *British Journal of Sociology* 51, no. 4 (December 2000): 605–22.

Hall, Wayne Michael, and Gary Citrenbaum. *Intelligence Analysis: How to Think in Complex Environments*. Santa Barbara, CA: Praeger Security International, 2010.

Hammerstrom, Michael L. "Intelligence and Military Operations." In *Intelligence and Military Operations*, edited by Michael I. Handel, 1–95. Portland, OR: Frank Cass, 1990.

———. "Leaders and Intelligence." In *Leaders and Intelligence*, edited by Michael I. Handel, 3–39. Totowa, NJ: Frank Cass, 1989.

———. "Size Matters: How Big Should a Military Design Team Be?" Unpublished monograph. Ft. Leavenworth, KS: School of Advanced Military Studies, 2010.

Handel, Michael I., ed. *Intelligence and Military Operations*. Portland, OR: Frank Cass, 1990.

———. *Leaders and Intelligence*. Totowa, NJ: Frank Cass, 1989.

Hart, B. H. Liddell. *Strategy*. 2nd revised ed. New York: Meridian Printing, 1991.

Hatlebrekke, Kjetil Anders, and M. L. R. Smith. "Towards a New Theory of Intelligence Failure? The Impact of Cognitive Closure and Discourse Failure." *Intelligence and National Security* 25, no. 2 (April 2010): 147–82.

Hebert, Adam J. "Compressing the Kill Chain." *Air Force Magazine*, March 2003, 50–54.

Heisenberg, Werner. *The Physical Principles of the Quantum Theory*. Translated by Carl Eckart and F. C. Hoyt. Mineola, NY: Dover Publications, Inc., 1949.

Herman, Michael. *Intelligence Services in the Information Age: Theory and Practice*. Portland, OR: Frank Cass, 2001.

Herodotus. *The Histories*. Translated by Robin Waterfield. New York: Oxford University Press, 1998.

Heuer, Richards J., Jr. *Psychology of Intelligence Analysis*. Washington, DC: Center for the Study of Intelligence, 1999.

Heuer, Richards J., Jr., and Randolph H. Pherson. *Structured Analytic Techniques for Intelligence Analysis*. Washington, DC: CQ Press, 2011.

Hinsley, Sir Harry. "World War II: An Intelligence Revolution." In *The Intelligence Revolution: A Historical Perspective*, edited by Lt Col Walter T. Hitchcock, 3–11. Washington, DC: US Government Printing Office, 1991.

Hitchcock, Walter T., ed. "The Intelligence Revolution: A Historical Perspective." *Proceedings of the Thirteenth Military History Symposium, US Air Force Academy*. Washington, DC: US Government Printing Office, 1988.

Hughes, Richard L., Robert C. Ginnett, and Gordon J. Curphy. *Leadership: Enhancing the Lessons of Experience*. 2nd ed. Chicago: Irwin, 1996.

Hughes-Wilson, John. *Military Intelligence Blunders*. New York: Carrol & Graf Publishers, 1999.

Hunt, E. Howard. *American Spy: My Secret History in the CIA, Watergate, and Beyond*. Hoboken, NJ: John Wiley & Sons, Inc., 2007.

Huntington, Samuel P. *The Soldier and the State: The Theory and Politics of Civil-Military Relations*. Cambridge, MA: Harvard University Press, 1957.

Jablonsky, David. "The Paradox of Duality: Adolf Hitler and the Concept of Military Surprise." In *Leaders and Intelligence*, edited by Michael I. Handel, 55–117. Totowa, NJ: Frank Cass, 1989.

Jervis, Robert. *Perception and Misperception in International Relations*. Princeton, NJ: Princeton University Press, 1976.

Johnson, Loch K. *Secret Agencies: US Intelligence in a Hostile World*. New Haven, CT: Yale University Press, 1996.

Joint Publication 2-0. *Joint Intelligence*, 22 June 2007.

Joint Publication 2-01. *Joint and National Intelligence Support to Military Operations*, 7 October 2004.

Joint Publication 2-01.3. *Joint Intelligence Preparation of the Operational Environment*, 16 June 2009.

Joint Publication 3-0. *Doctrine for Joint Operations*, 10 September 2001.

———. *Joint Operations, change 2*, 22 March 2010.

Joint Publication 5-0. *Joint Operation Planning*, 26 December 2006.

Jomini, Antoine-Henri. *The Art of War*. Translated by G. H. Mendell and W. P. Craighill. Mineola, NY: Dover Publications, 2007.

Jones, R. V. "Intelligence and Command." In *Leaders and Intelligence*, edited by Michael I. Handel, 288–98. Totowa, NJ: Frank Cass, 1989.

Kahn, David. *The Codebreakers: The Story of Secret Writing*. New York: MacMillan Publishing Co., Inc., 1967.

———. "An Historical Theory of Intelligence." In *Intelligence Theory: Key Questions and Debates*, edited by Peter Gill, Stephen Marrin, and Mark Pythian, 4–15. New York: Routledge, 2009.

Keegan, John. *Intelligence in War: The Value—and Limitations—of What the Military Can Learn about the Enemy*. New York: Vintage Books, 2002.

Kelly, Justin, and Mike Brennan. *Alien: How Operational Art Devoured Strategy*. Carlisle, PA: Strategic Studies Institute, 2009.

Kem, Jack D. *Design: Tools of the Trade*. Ft. Leavenworth, KS: US Army Combined Arms Center, May 2009.

Kennett, Lee. *The First Air War, 1914–1918*. New York: Free Press, 1991.

Kent, Sherman. *Strategic Intelligence for American World Policy*. 2nd ed. Princeton, NJ: Princeton University Press, 1949/1966.

Kiras, James D. "Irregular Warfare: Terrorism and Insurgency." In *Understanding Modern Warfare*, by David Jordan, James D. Kiras, David J. Lonsdale, Ian Speller, and Christopher Tuck, 225–91. Cambridge, UK: Cambridge University Press, 2008.

Kitson, Frank. *Low Intensity Operations: Subversion, Insurgency, Peacekeeping*. St. Petersburg, FL: Hailer Publishing, 2005.

Klein, Gary A. *The Power of Intuition: How to Use Your Gut Feelings to Make Better Decisions at Work*. New York: Currency, 2004.

Knightley, Phillip. *The Second Oldest Profession: Spies and Spying in the Twentieth Century*. New York: W. W. Norton, 1986.

Koch, Oscar W., and Robert G. Hays. *G–2: Intelligence for Patton*. Philadelphia, PA: Whitmore Publishing Co., 1971.

Komer, R. W. *The Malayan Emergency in Retrospect: Organization of a Successfull Counterinsurgency Effort*. Memorandum R-957-ARPA. Santa Monica, CA: RAND Corporation, February 1972.

Kruglanski, Arie W. *Lay Epistemics and Human Knowledge: Cognitive and Motivated Biases*. New York: Plenum, 1989.

Kuhn, Thomas S. *The Structure of Scientific Revolutions*. 3rd ed. Chicago: University of Chicago Press, 1996.

Laqueur, Walter. *A World of Secrets: The Uses and Limits of Intelligence*. New York: Basic Books, 1985.

Lawson, Bryan. *How Designers Think: The Design Process Demystified*. 4th ed. Burlington, MA: Architectural Press, 2006.

LeGault, Michael R. *Think!: Why Crucial Decisions Can't Be Made in the Blink of an Eye*. New York: Threshold Editions, 2006.

Levite, Ariel. *Intelligence and Strategic Surprises*. New York: Columbia University Press, 1987.

Libicki, Martin C. "DBK and Its Consequences." In *Dominant Battlespace Knowledge: The Winning Edge*, edited by Stuart E. Johnson and Martin C. Libicki, 27–58. Washington, DC: National Defense University Press Publications, 1995.

———. "Information War, Information Peace." *Journal of International Affairs* 51, no. 2 (Spring 1998): 411–28.

———. *The Mesh and the Net: Speculations on Armed Conflict in a Time of Free Silicon*. McNair Paper 28, Institute for National Strategic Studies. Washington, DC: National Defense University, March 1995.

Lindley, Dennis V. *Understanding Uncertainty*. Hoboken, NJ: Wiley-Interscience, 2006.

Lowenthal, Mark M. *Intelligence: From Secrets to Policy*. 4th ed. Washington, DC: CQ Press, 2009.

Luttwak, Edward N. "The Operational Level of War." *International Security* 5, no. 3 (Winter 1980–1981): 61–79.

Luvaas, Jay. "Napoleon's Use of Intelligence: The Jena Campaign of 1805." In *Leaders and Intelligence*, edited by Michael I. Handel, 40–54. Totowa, NJ: Frank Cass, 1989.

Lyttelton, Oliver. *The Memoirs of Lord Chandos*. London: Bodley Head, 1962.

MacLachlan, Donald. *Intelligence: The Common Denominator*. Vol. I. In *The Fourth Dimension of Warfare: Intelligence, Subversion, Resistance*, edited by Michael Eliot Bateman. Manchester, England: Manchester University Press, 1970.

Mahnken, Thomas G. *Technology and the American Way of War since 1945*. New York: Columbia University Press, 2008.

Mangio, Charles A., and Bonnie J. Wilkinson. "Intelligence Analysis: Once Again." Interim report. Wright-Patterson AFB, OH: Air Force Research Laboratory, 2008.

Maslowski, Peter. "Military Intelligence Sources during the American Civil War: A Case Study." In *The Intelligence Revolution; A Historical Perspective: Proceedings of the Thirteenth Military History Symposium, US Air Force Academy, Colorado Springs, Colorado, October 12-14, 1988*, edited by the US Air Force Academy Office of Military History, 39–59. Washington, DC: United States Air Force, 1991.

Mattis, James N. "USJFCOM Commander's Guidance for Effects-Based Operations." *Parameters* 38, no. 3 (Autumn 2008): 18–25.

———. "Vision for a Joint Approach to Operational Design." US Joint Forces Command. Accessed 29 April 2011. http://www.jfcom.mil/newslink/storyarchive/2009/aod_2009.pdf.

May, Ernest R. "Capabilities and Proclivities." In *Knowing One's Enemies: Intelligence Assessment before the Two World Wars*, edited by Ernest R. May, 503–41. Princeton, NJ: Princeton University Press, 1984.

———. "Introduction." In *Knowing One's Enemies: Intelligence Assessment before the Two World Wars*, edited by Ernest R. May, 3–8. Princeton, NJ: Princeton University Press, 1984.

———, ed. *Knowing One's Enemies: Intelligence Assessment before the Two World Wars*. Princeton, NJ: Princeton University Press, 1984.

McGlade, Patrick E. "Effects-Based Operations Versus Systemic Operational Design: Is There a Difference?" Graduate research paper. Wright-Patterson AFB, OH: Air Force Institute of Technology, June 2006.

McHenry, David P. "Battle Command: An Approach to Wickedness." Unpublished monograph. Ft. Leavenworth, KS: School of Advanced Military Studies, 21 May 2009.

Meilinger, Phillip S. "A History of Effects-Based Air Operations." *Journal of Military History* 71, no. 1 (January 2007): 139–68.

Merton, Robert K. "The Matthew Effect in Science." *Science* 159, no. 3819 (January 1968): 56–63.

Moore, David T. *Critical Thinking and Intelligence Analysis*. Washington, DC: Center for Strategic Intelligence Research, 2006.

Murray, Williamson, and Allan R. Millett. "Introduction: Military Effectiveness Twenty Years After." In *Military Effectiveness*, edited by Allan R. Millett and Williamson Murray. Vol. 3, *The Second World War*, xi–xix. New York: Cambridge University Press, 2010.

Murray, Williamson, and Allan R. Millett, eds. *Military Effectiveness*. Vol. 3, *The Second World War*. New York: Cambridge University Press, 2010.

Nagl, John A. *Learning to Eat Soup with a Knife: Counterinsurgency Lessons from Malaya and Vietnam*. Chicago: University of Chicago Press, 2005.

Naval Doctrine Publication 2. *Naval Intelligence*. n. d.

Naveh, Shimon. *In Pursuit of Military Excellence: The Evolution of Operational Theory*. New York: Frank Cass, 1997.

Nelson, Theodor. *Computer Lib*. Seattle, WA: Microsoft Press, 1987.

Neustadt, Richard. *Presidential Power*. New York: Wiley, 1980.

Neustadt, Richard E., and Ernest R. May. *Thinking in Time: The Use of History for Decision Makers*. New York: Free Press, 1986.

Norris, Pat. *Spies in the Sky: Surveillance Satellites in War and Peace*. New York: Springer Praxis Books, 2007.

Norwitz, Jeffrey H. "Leveraging Operational Intelligence: The Battle of Tannenberg and Masurian Lakes, 1914." Unpublished monograph. Newport, RI: Naval War College, 14 May 2001.

Nye, Joseph S. "Peering into the Future." *Foreign Affairs* 73, no. 4 (July/August 1994): 82–93.

Nye, Roger H. *The Patton Mind: The Professional Development of an Extraordinary Leader*. Garden City Park, NY: Avery Publishing, 1993.

Owens, William A. "The Emerging System of Systems." *Military Review* 75, no. 3 (May/June 1995): 15.

Parkenham, Thomas. *The Boer War*. New York: Random House, 1979.

Pateman, Roy. *Residual Uncertainty: Trying to Avoid Intelligence and Policy Mistakes in the Modern World*. Lanham, MD: University Press of America, 2003.

Perrow, Charles. *Normal Accidents: Living with High-Risk Technologies*. Princeton, NJ: Princeton University Press, 1999.

Popper, Karl R. *The Logic of Scientific Discovery*. New York: Routledge Classics, 2005.

———. *The Open Society and Its Enemies*. Vol. 2, *Hegel and Marx*. London: Routledge, 2003.

Porter, Patrick. *Military Orientalism: Eastern War through Western Eyes*. New York: Columbia University Press, 2009.

Posen, Barry R. *The Sources of Military Doctrine: France, Britain, and Germany between the World Wars*. Ithaca, NY: Cornell University Press, 1984.

Powers, Thomas. *Intelligence Wars: American Secret History from Hitler to al-Qaeda*. New York: New York Review Books, 2002.

Purcell, Victor. *Malaya: Communist or Free?* London: Victor Gollancz, 1954.

Pye, Lucian W. *Guerrilla Communism in Malaya: Its Social and Political Meaning*. Princeton, NJ: Princeton University Press, 1956.

Ramakrishna, Kumar. "Content, Credibility and Context: Propaganda Government Surrender Policy and the Malayan Communist Terrorist Mass Surrenders of 1958." *Intelligence and National Security* 14, no. 4 (Winter 1999): 242–66.

———. "'Transmogrifying' Malaya: the Impact of Sir Gerald Templer (1952-54)." *Journal of Southeast Asian Studies* 32, no. 1 (February 2001): 79–92.

Ransom, Harry Howe. "The Politicization of Intelligence." In *Strategic Intelligence: Windows into a Secret World*, edited by Loch K. Johnson and James J. Wirtz, 171–82. Los Angeles: Roxbury Publishing Company, 2004.

Reilly, Jeffrey M. *Operational Design: Shaping Decision Analysis through Cognitive Vision*. Maxwell AFB, AL: Air Command and Staff College, 2009.

Rittel, Horst W. J., and Melvin M. Webber. "Dilemmas in a General Theory of Planning." *Policy Sciences* 4, no. 2 (1973): 155–69.

Rose, Alexander. *Washington's Spies: The Story of America's First Spy Ring.* New York: Bantam, 2006.

Rosello, Victor M. "Clausewitz's Contempt for Intelligence." In *Intelligence and the National Security Strategist*, edited by Roger Z. George and Robert D. Kline, 11–20. Lanham, MD: Rowman & Littlefield Publishers, Inc., 2006.

Rosen, Stephen R. *Winning the Next War: Innovation and the Modern Military.* Ithaca, NY: Cornell University Press, 2001.

Rosenau, James N. "Many Damn Things Simultaneously: Complexity Theory and World Affairs." In *Complexity, Global Politics and National Security*, edited by David S. Alberts and Thomas J. Czerwinski, 32–43. Washington, DC: National Defense University, 1997.

Ruby, Tomislav Z. "Effects-Based Operations: More Important Than Ever." *Parameters* 38, no. 3 (Autumn 2008): 26–35.

Ruffner, Kevin C., ed. *CORONA: America's First Satellite Program.* Washington, DC: Center for the Study of Intelligence, 1995.

Ryan, Alexander. *Art of Design, Student Text Version 2.0.* Ft. Leavenworth, KS: School of Advanced Military Studies, 2010.

Schmitt, John F. "Command and (Out of) Control: The Military Implications of Complexity Theory." In *Complexity, Global Politics and National Security*, edited by David S. Alberts and Thomas J. Czerwinski, 99–111. Washington, DC: National Defense University, 1997.

———. "A Systemic Concept for Operational Design." Air University. Accesssed 10 December 2010. http://www.au.af.mil/au/awc/awcgate/usmc/mcwl_schmitt_op_design.pdf.

Schön, Donald A. *The Reflective Practitioner: How Professionals Think in Action.* London: Temple Smith, 1983.

Senge, Peter. *The Fifth Discipline: The Art and Practice of the Learning Organization.* 2nd ed. New York: Currency, 2006.

Shannon, Claude E. "A Mathematical Theory of Communication." *Bell System Technical Journal* 27 (July and October 1948): 379–423, 623–56.

Short, Anthony. "Communism and the Emergency." In *Malaysia: A Survey*, edited by Wang Gungwu, 149–60. New York: Praeger, 1964.

———. *The Communist Insurrection in Malaya 1948–1960.* London: Frederick Muller, 1975.

Showalter, Dennis E. "Intelligence on the Eve of Transformation: Methodology, Organization, and Application." In *The Intelligence Revolution: A Historical Perspective*, edited by Lt Col Walter T. Hitchcock, 15–37. Washington, DC: US Government Printing Office, 1988.

Shulsky, Abram N. *Silent Warfare: Understanding the World of Intelligence.* 3rd ed. Washington, DC: Brassey's, 2002.

Shwedo, Bradford J. *XIX Tactical Air Command and ULTRA: Patton's Force Enhancers in the 1944 Campaign in France.* Cadre Paper no. 10. Maxwell AFB, AL: Air University Press, May 2001.

Simpkin, Richard. *Deep Battle: The Brainchild of Marshal Tukhachevskii.* McLean, VA: Pergamon-Brassey's International Defense Publishers, 1987.

Slim, William. *Defeat into Victory.* London: Cassell, 1972.

Smith, Simon C. "General Templer and Counter-Insurgency in Malaya: Hearts and Minds, Intelligence and Propaganda." *Intelligence and National Security* 16, no. 3 (Autumn 2001): 60–78.

Sorrells, William T., Glen R. Downing, Paul J. Blakesley, David W. Pendall, Jason K. Walk, and Richard D. Wallwork. "Systemic Operational Design: An Introduction." Unpublished monograph. Ft. Leavenworth, KS: School of Advanced Military Studies, 26 May 2005.

Spinuzzi, Marc A. "CCIR for Complex and Uncertain Environments." Unpublished monograph. Ft. Leavenworth, KS: School of Advanced Military Studies, 1 May 2007.

Stewart, Brian. "Winning in Malaya: An Intelligence Success Story." *Intelligence and National Security* 14, no. 4 (Winter 1999): 267–83.

Stockwell, A. J., ed. *British Documents on the End of Empire: Malaya. Part I, The Malayan Union Experiment, 1942–1948.* London: HMSO Books, 1995.

———. *British Documents on the End of Empire: Malaya. Part II, The Communist Insurrection, 1948–1953.* London: HMSO Books, 1995.

———. "British Imperial Policy and Decolonisation in Malaya, 1942-52." *Journal of Imperial and Commonwealth History* 13, no. 1 (1984): 68–87.

———. "Insurgency and Decolonisation during the Malayan Emergency." *Journal of Commonwealth & Comparative Politics* 25, no. 1 (1987): 71–81.

Stubbs, Richard. *Hearts and Minds in Guerrilla Warfare: The Malayan Emergency 1948–1960.* Singapore: Eastern Universities Press, 2004.

Sunderland, Riley. "Antiguerrilla Intelligence in Malaya, 1948–1960." Memorandum RM-4172-ISA. Santa Monica, CA: RAND Corporation, September 1964.

Thomas, David. "U.S. Military Intelligence Analysis: Old and New Challenges." In *Analyzing Intelligence: Origins, Obstacles, and Innovations,* edited by Roger Z. George and James B. Bruce, 138–54. Washington, DC: Georgetown University Press, 2008.

Thompson, Sir Robert. *Defeating Communist Insurgency: The Lessons of Malaya and Vietnam.* St. Petersburg, FL: Hailer Publishing, 2005.

Thucydides. *The Landmark Thucydides: A Comprehensive Guide to the Peloponnesian War.* Edited by Robert B. Strassler. New York: Simon & Schuster, 1998.

Treverton, Gregory F. "Intelligence Analysis: Between 'Politicization' and Irrelevance." In *Analyzing Intelligence: Origins, Obstacles, and Innovations,* edited by Roger Z. George and James B. Bruce, 91–104. Washington, DC: Georgetown University Press, 2007.

Turner, Stansfield. *Burn before Reading: Presidents, CIA Directors, and Secret Intelligence.* New York: Hyperion, 2005.

Tzu, Sun. *The Illustrated Art of War.* Translated by Samuel B. Griffith. New York: Oxford University Press, 2005.

Ulmer, Jr., Walter F. "Military Leadership into the 21st Century: Another Bridge Too Far?' " *Parameters* 28, no. 1 (Spring 1998): 4–25.

US Army Training and Doctrine Command (TRADOC) Pamphlet 525-5-500. *Commander's Appreciation and Campaign Design, Version 1.0.,* 28 January 2008.

US Joint Forces Command. *Design in Military Operations: A Primer for Joint Warfighters.* Joint Doctrine Series Pamphlet 10. Norfolk, VA: Joint Warfighting Center, 20 September 2010.

———. *Operational Implications of Effects-Based Operations.* Joint Doctrine Series Pamphlet 7. Norfolk, VA: Joint Warfighting Center,17 November 2004.

Van Creveld, Martin L. *Command in War.* Cambridge, MA: Harvard University Press, 1985.

Vego, Milan N. "A Case against Systemic Operational Design." *Joint Force Quarterly,* no. 53 (April 2009): 69–75.

Waldrop, M. Mitchell. *Complexity: The Emerging Science at the Edge of Order and Chaos.* New York: Simon & Schuster, 1992.

Warner, Michael. "Wanted: A Definition of Intelligence." *Studies in Intelligence* 46, no. 3 (2002): 15–22.

Weigley, Russell F. "The Political and Strategic Dimensions of Military Effectiveness." In *Military Effectiveness,* edited by Allan R. Millett and Williamson Murray. Vol. 3, *The Second World War,* 341–64. New York: Cambridge University Press, 2010.

Westerfield, H. Bradford. "Inside Ivory Bunkers: CIA Analysts Resist Managers' 'Pandering.'" In *Strategic Intelligence: Windows into a Secret World,* edited by Loch K. Johnson and James J. Wirtz, 198–218. Los Angeles: Roxbury Publishing Company, 2004.

Wiener, Norbert. *The Human Use of Human Beings: Cybernetics and Society.* New York: Anchor Books, 1954.

Winterbotham, F. W. *The ULTRA Secret.* London: Dell, 1975.

Winton, Harold R. "Strategy, Operational Art, and Tactics: A Historical Perspective." Lecture. School of Advanced Air and Space Studies, Maxwell AFB, AL, 2010.

Wirtz, James J. "Intelligence to Please? The Order of Battle Controversy During the Vietnam War." In *Strategic Intelligence: Windows into a Secret World*, edited by Loch K. Johnson and James J. Wirtz, 183–97. Los Angeles: Roxbury Publishing Company, 2004.